Alice Edwards Pratt

The Use of Color in the Verse of the English Romantic Poets

Alice Edwards Pratt

The Use of Color in the Verse of the English Romantic Poets

ISBN/EAN: 9783744673877

Printed in Europe, USA, Canada, Australia, Japan

Cover: Foto ©Thomas Meinert / pixelio.de

More available books at **www.hansebooks.com**

THE USE OF COLOR

IN THE

VERSE OF THE ENGLISH ROMANTIC POETS

BY

ALICE EDWARDS PRATT

CHICAGO

The University of Chicago Press

1898

TABLE OF CONTENTS

	PAGE
INTRODUCTION	v
BIBLIOGRAPHY	x
CHAPTER I Langland, Gower, Chaucer, Spenser, Milton	1
CHAPTER II Pope	14
CHAPTER III Thomson	23
CHAPTER IV Gray, Goldsmith, Cowper	33
CHAPTER V Scott	38
CHAPTER VI Coleridge	46
CHAPTER VII Wordsworth	52
CHAPTER VIII Byron	61
CHAPTER IX Shelley	69
CHAPTER X Keats	78
CONCLUSION: General Plan	89
i Color-Vocabulary	90
ii Color-Scale	95
iii Color-Distribution	97
INDIVIDUAL AND COMPARATIVE VOCABULARIES	103
TABLES AND CHARTS	114

iii

INTRODUCTION.

The use of color in literature has, in the last half century, attracted the attention of many eminent scientists. Philologist, anthropologist, and physicist have alike found in this subject a fruitful field for investigation. As yet, however, study has been largely confined to ancient writings such as the *Rig-Veda*, the *Zend Avesta*, the *Iliad*, and the *Æneid;* and the character of these investigations may be inferred from the fact that the results have been published chiefly in philological and anthropological journals.[1] The possible æsthetic value of such study, and its significance in the interpretation of the author himself, have been but cursorily touched upon; while the color-terms of modern English poets have never received serious treatment.

A few brief articles or sections of articles on this latter division of the subject have, it is true, been published within the past twenty years; but Mr. Grant Allen's book on *The Colour Sense* is written from the anthropologist's point of view, and devotes only a few pages to the English poets. E. W. Hopkins, in an article on "Words for Colour in the Rig-Veda" (*American Journal of Philology*, 1883), has mentioned the color-range of the *Paradise Lost* as essentially the same as that of the *Rig-Veda*. The only deliberate attempt to examine and compare the color-terms of English and other poets, made from an æsthetic and literary point of view, is that of Mr. Havelock Ellis in the *Contemporary Review*, May, 1896, filling sixteen pages, and ranging rapidly over a broad and varied field, from the *Völsunga Saga* and Isaiah to Pater and Olive Schreiner. Mr. Ellis's article is extremely interesting, and, to the average reader, full of suggestive stimulus. At the time of its appearance, however, the

[1] The discussion of the point raised by Mr. Gladstone (*loc. cit.*, p. 367), that color was little known to the ancients and that the sense of it has been gradually developed, is well summed up by Mr. Lubbock (*loc. cit.*).

tables and charts upon which this thesis is based—the work of
four years' reading and computation—were just completed;
and a comparison of the results here printed, upon those points
in which these investigations and Mr. Ellis's coincide, will show
how unscientific are his methods, and how unsupported many of
his deductions. A fuller examination of some of the inaccura-
cies into which he has been led by generalizing from insufficient
data will be found in the chapter of this thesis devoted to Thomson, since in the case of this poet Mr. Ellis has stated exactly
what poems he used, and can therefore be followed in his deductions; meanwhile, it may be safely said that the field which this
thesis aims to cover in part is, up to this time, an untouched one.
It has not, however, remained untouched for lack of suggestive-
ness in the subject. The sense-perceptions possessed by the
great English poets, the relative keenness of sight, hearing, and
smell in the poetic nature, the possible development of one of
these faculties above the other in the course of generations—
all these questions have for years been matters of lively interest
to psychologists as well as to students of English literature.

The present study of color as it appears in English poetry
has for its chief field the verse of the Romantic Period, as found
in the works of Scott, Coleridge, Wordsworth, Byron, Shelley,
and Keats.

To trace the use which Victorian poets have made of their
rich heritage of color, to see what new possibilities they have discovered in old color-terms, or what additional terms they have
adopted from prose or minted for themselves, would be a task
both delightful and profitable. It does not, however, lie within
the scope of the present paper.

But, while color in poets later than the Romanticists is omitted
from consideration here, its treatment by representative English
poets of preceding centuries has been studied in order that a
more intelligent view might be taken of the Romanticists themselves. Knowing the color-vocabularies of a man's masters and
the associations which certain hues have probably gained for him
through his reading, we may the better understand at what point
he takes his departure from customary usages, where he shows

the greatest originality in his use of hues, and where, in the world of color, his chief interest lies.

Langland, Gower, Chaucer, Spenser, Shakspere, Milton, Pope, Thomson, Gray, Goldsmith, and Cowper furnish examples of all species of verse, except the ballad. In their work we have the purely didactic narrative, the dramatic narrative, the allegorical narrative; there we have the drama, both classic and romantic, and the greater epic; there also satirical verse in the form of the humorous burlesque or of the lashing invective; there pastorals in both the Theocritean and the Virgilian manners; there delicate Nature lyrics and straightforward Nature descriptions; there odes and elegies, marriage hymns and impassioned love sonnets. A survey of the color-vocabulary of these poets ought, therefore, to yield us about all of the terms used to denote hue in English verse up to the time of Wordsworth. And a study of the manner in which each of these earlier poets used his colors, and of the fields to which he applied them, ought to give us an ample background for the study of the members of the Romantic School as colorists.

The entire amount of English verse written by each of the seventeen poets named, including all dramas written in verse with the exception of Thomson's, has been studied in the best available texts,[1] and each usage of color has been catalogued. The results for each poet have been classified in two ways: first, according color-groups; second, according to distribution among the various fields of interest.

In the first classification I have made nine groups: Reds, Yellows, Browns, Greens, Blues, Purples, Whites, Grays, Blacks. The color-vocabularies of the several poets, classified according to these groups, with mention of the number of times each word appears, will be found chronologically arranged on pp. 103–10. Tables I, II, III present numerical summaries of the vocabularies thus classified; and Tables IV and V show in order of preference, as determined by usage, each poet's leading words, and his color-scale according to groups.

[1] In the case of Shakspere, Schmidt's *Shakspere Lexicon* and Bartlett's *Concordance* were used instead of the text.

In the second classification, in order to show how color is distributed in the worlds of men and of matter, I have arranged the poets' color-usages under twelve heads, each of which (excepting K, which is miscellaneous) represents a special field of interest. These heads are represented in my tables by letters as follows: A, man; B, dress; C, manufactured articles; D, animals; E, minerals; F, flowers and fruits; G, the sky; H, the land; I, the waters; K, objects miscellaneous and indefinite; X, color as color; Z, abstractions. A fuller explanation of each class will be found on p. 113, following which are Tables VI, VII, VIII, IX, and Charts A and B, all summarizing, though in a variety of ways, the results of the classification of colors according to fields of interest.

In the cataloguing and classifying of terms, many minor difficulties have been encountered. Broadly speaking, these difficulties are of three classes, each of which may be represented by a question: 1) Does this word signify color at all? 2) To which of the nine color-groups does it belong? 3) Under what field of application does it fall?

The first question arises when the term has more than one meaning and we are in doubt as to which the poet intended. For instance, when Shelley says, " Look on yonder earth. The golden harvests spring" (*Mab*, III, 193), are we to define "golden" as yellow in color, or wealth-producing? And when Keats calls Apollo

> God of the golden bow,
> And of the golden lyre,
> And of the golden hair,
> And of the golden fire
>
> (*Hymn to Apollo*, 1–4),

shall we say that in the last two lines he uses "golden" as a synonym of bright yellow, but in the first two lines thinks of the metal only and not its shine?

The second question is provoked by hues which lie on the border line between color-groups. For example, is "creamy" to be classed with Whites or Yellows; "tawny," with Yellows or Browns; "dun," with Browns or Blacks?

The difficulties coming under the third class are by far the most troublesome. Take the following instance. Scott says that the war horse

> Champs till both bit and boss are white.
> —*Lord of the Isles*, I, xv, 12.

Now when we have class C for the colors of manufactured articles, and D for animal hues, and I for all forms of water, including foam, where ought we to place this particular "white"?

Such questions must be met in every poet's color; but the proportion of doubtful or troublesome words is, after all, so slight in comparison with the great body of definite and definitely applied hue that I trust that any misjudgment on my part in including or placing them will not vitiate my results. In the case of Shakspere, however, I would beg especial indulgence, since I have not attempted to study his hues in their contexts, but present here only what can be culled from concordances.

Outside the results drawn, in this one case, from concordances, I have examined and tabulated some four hundred thousand lines of verse. But even from a mass of data so large as this I shall not attempt to draw general conclusions of the sort which Mr. Havelock Ellis has put forward. I shall not speak of the renewal of interest in white, or of the lack of appreciation of blue, in any one period. Such things seem rather matters of individual preference than general tendencies, and, despite the apparent exactness of figures and percentages, allowance must always be made, in this sort of work, for the personal equation. It is this consideration which has urged the writing of separate chapters on the Romanticists, and on, Pope and Thomson.

The centralization of this study upon the Romantic poets will need no justification, especially after an inspection of Charts A and B has shown the union of the two great streams of color-interest which takes place in that school.

BIBLIOGRAPHY.

Allen, Grant: *The Colour Sense.* Trübner, 1879.

Ballerstedt, E.: *Ueber Chaucers Naturschilderungen.* Göttingen, 1891.

Blumner, Hugo: *Die Farbenzeichnungen bei den römischen Dichtern.* Berlin, 1892.

Brandl, Alois: *S. T. Coleridge and the English Romantic School.* Translated by Lady Eastlake. Murray, 1887.

Browne, William Hand: "Color Chords in Thomson's 'Seasons,'" *Modern Language Notes,* May, 1897.

Colvin, Sidney: *Keats* ("English Men of Letters"). Macmillan, 1890.

Dowden, Edward: *Life of Shelley.* Kegan Paul, Trübner & Co., 1896.

Ellis, Havelock: "The Color Sense in Literature," *Contemporary Review,* May, 1896.

Garnett, Richard: *The Poetical Works of Coleridge* ("The Muses Library"). Lawrence & Bullen, 1897.

Gladstone, W. E.: "The Colour-Sense," *Nineteenth Century,* October, 1877.

Hopkins, E. W.: "Words for Color in the Rig-Veda," *American Journal of Philology,* IV, p. 167, 1883.

Lubbock, Montagu: "The Development of the Colour-Sense," *Fortnightly,* Vol. XXXV, 1882.

Masson, David: *Wordsworth, Shelley, and Keats.* Macmillan, 1875.

Price, Thomas R.: "The Color System of Vergil," *American Journal of Philology,* IV, 1883.

Reynolds, Myra: *The Treatment of Nature in English Poetry between Pope and Wordsworth.* University of Chicago Press, 1896.

Ruskin, John: *Modern Painters.* New York, 1878.

NOTE.—The poetical texts used are noted at the opening of the chapters on the separate authors. Books named above are those to which reference has been made in the text.

CHAPTER I.

I. LANGLAND'S USE OF COLOR.

Text used : *Piers the Plowman* (B) and *Richard the Redeless.* Skeat edition.
2 vols. Oxford, 1886.
Number of lines, 8,032.
For vocabulary see p. 103.

II. GOWER'S USE OF COLOR.

Text used : *Confessio Amantis.* Dr. R. Pauli's edition. 3 vols. Bell & Daldy,
1857.
Number of lines, 33,704.
For vocabulary see p. 104.

III. CHAUCER'S USE OF COLOR.

Text used : *Complete Works.* Skeat edition. 1 vol. Macmillan, 1895.
Number of lines, 34,109.
For vocabulary see p. 104.

IV. SPENSER'S USE OF COLOR.

Text used : *Complete Works.* Globe edition. Macmillan, 1890.
Number of lines, 45,553.
For vocabulary see p. 104.

V. MILTON'S USE OF COLOR.

Text used : *Poetical Works.* 1 vol. Lovell Co.
Number of lines, 16,987.
For vocabulary see p. 105.

NOTE.—Shakspere is not separately treated in the text. For his vocabulary see p. 105.

LANGLAND, GOWER, CHAUCER, SPENSER, MILTON.

In the work of Chaucer, Gower, and Langland we have represented, with some measure of completeness, the two extremes
of English verse and of English social conditions in the four-

teenth century. While the entire poetic production of Chaucer and the *Confessio Amantis* of Gower represent the conscious cultured endeavor of men writing for pure æsthetic pleasure, Langland speaks with a single intensity of purpose : his aim is censure and reform. The subjects and the meters of the two former poets are taken from foreign literary models; but Langland's thoughts, sympathies, and verse-form are strictly English.

From a knowledge of only the external facts about these three poets we might anticipate some of their characteristics as colorists. The descriptive and narrative character of the work of Chaucer and Gower promises a varied and perhaps liberal use of color in their verse, while their acquaintance with French literature opens to them the entire Romance vocabulary in addition to their own. In the same way, the limitations of Langland's purpose, the homiletic tone he adopts, and the restriction of his reading, presuppose a scanty and subdued coloring, its terms chosen from those current among the people to whom he addresses himself.

I.

Piers the Plowman (B text) and *Richard the Redeless* give together a total of 8,032 lines, in which there are 32 references to color. (See p. 103.) The leading features of this vocabulary become evident at a glance. It is extremely simple, and, with the exception of " enblaunched " and " pale," wholly Teutonic. Not only are its terms common and current, but they occur in most cases under such circumstances that the use of hue seems more formal than intentional on the poet's part, *i. e.*, twenty-five of the thirty-two color-usages carry the alliteration, and four more are mere phrases. The colors most frequently used are red, green, and white.

Langland's vocabulary is not only simple, but also defective in range. It contains no yellow, no golden, no brown, and no real blue, for "blo" as used by him means "livid "—O. N. *blār*, not O. Fr. *bleu*.

The poet's range of color-application is also narrow. Almost without exception he applies his coloring to man and to objects closely associated with man, especially to the latter field, in his brief descriptions of clothing, ornaments, or food. There is no nearer approach to the coloring of external Nature than is found in the "grene" of *Piers Plowman*, XV, 100. Red is the term which he seems to use with most deliberate color-intent, as will appear from his one and only passage of vivid coloring, the description of Meed in *Piers Plowman*, II, 7-18.

Our anticipations with regard to Langland are thus fully borne out by examination of his verse. We find his color-terms few, popularly current, and often indeterminate. Such interest as he evinces in this field is all turned towards Man rather than Nature; and either the strength of his moral purpose or the limitation of his subject has barred out any attempt at decorative effect.

II.

The *Confessio Amantis* of John Gower stands, as regards subject-matter, on a par with Chaucer's work, and draws largely upon Ovid for its narrative detail. Knowing as we do that Gower was versed enough in the French language to compose one presumably long poem in that tongue, we might fairly expect that his vocabulary and his numerical color-average would show a marked advance over Langland, and would nearly resemble those of his brother-poet Chaucer. But an examination of the 33,704 short lines of the *Confessio Amantis* shows that Gower takes from the Romance languages only 4 of his 15 color-terms, as contrasted with Chaucer's 17 Romance words out of 42. Despite his extensive borrowings from Ovid, he transfers to his pages none of the Latin poet's color, and his vocabulary is almost as simply Teutonic as is that of Langland. Nor does his color-average per 1,000 lines show much advance on that of *Piers Plowman*.

But if Gower rarely goes beyond the simple Teutonic color-vocabulary found in Langland's work, and if he lays on his color with a hand almost as sparing, he shows in the terms which he uses most frequently, and in the distribution of his hues, the influence of Romance writers—of Ovid, and of the authors of the *Roman de la Rose.* This influence causes an apparent emphasis on the green of the peaceful landscape in the *Confessio Amantis,* and brings green up numerically to the first place in Gower's list of preferred colors; for Gower, following the choice of the French poets, takes the verdant month of May and the May landscape as the background of his narrative. When we include his neutral hues, however, we see that the greater part of Gower's color is applied to Man. He does not make this application as did Langland; his allusions to attire are very few indeed; but he expends his color upon the human body itself, and dwells with evident pleasure on the hair, eyes, and complexion of his characters. Typical descriptions by Gower of womanly beauty may be found in the *Confessio Amantis,* II, p. 210, and III, p. 27. It may be noted that he, like Chaucer, observes the traces of emotion in the countenance, as marked by a changing hue.

Gower thus occupies, as a colorist, a position intermediate between Langland and Chaucer. The former he resembles in his simple and limited vocabulary and in his small color-average, less than four words per 1,000 lines; the latter he approaches at those points where both show the influence of Romance models; viz.: in the manner of describing human beings, especially beautiful women, and in the abundant use of the green of springtime. Even his most vivid bits of coloring, however, have an air of polite artificiality, and impress us as mere Romance adornments which he has borrowed along with his stories.

III.

The color-vocabulary of Chaucer may seem limited when compared with that of Elizabethan writers, yet its 42 terms are a striking advance upon Langland's 12 and Gower's 15. Chaucer omits only 4 of the hues used by his two contemporaries, and adds 30, among which are conspicuous the names of dye-stuffs and of colored cloths — a fact quite in keeping with his interest in the dress of his men and women. Despite the large number of Romance color-terms which he employs — 17 out of 42 — the emphasis of usage, as in Gower, remains upon the simple primitive words. There are 10 words in his vocabulary for red, but the old "rede" appears in 79 out of the 100 usages of the color; there are also 10 words for white, but they are so distributed that "whyt" and "pale" occur 125 times, and the remaining 8 terms taken together only 29 times. "Yelw" and "gold" count together for 22 of the 34 uses of Yellows, and "blak" for 58 of the 61 Blacks. Green and brown have no synonyms; and despite the frequent occurrence of "verdure," "vermeille," and "blanche" in the *Roman de la Rose*, Chaucer renders these words by the simple terms "green," "red" or "ruddy," and "white," neither here nor elsewhere using "verdant" or "vermeil." His vocabulary shows a marked advance over Gower's in the use of color symbolically: "white" of purity and innocence; "black" of the sorrowful or mysterious; "hoar" of age, decrepitude, and ruin; "blue" or "azure" of truth and steadfastness (*Sq. T.*, 635–7; *Anel.*, 330–32; *Tr. and Cr.*, III, 884); and "green" occasionally of fickleness (*Anel.*, 180; *Sq. T.*, 638–9).

Two factors tend to qualify Chaucer's originality and independence in the use of color. A comparison of Fragment A of the *Romaunt of the Rose* with the original French, as printed by Skeat in Vol. I of his monumental edition of Chaucer, will show in how many cases color-terms and descriptive formulæ in Chaucer's work may be traced to a possible French source. Space forbids full discussion of the matter here; but the question is an interesting one. The other possible limitation of his color-individuality is the frequency with which the commoner terms appear in rime. "White," "red," "green," and "black," his four most frequent color-words, furnish 132 out of his 165 color-rimes, *i. e.*, rimes in which one of the two words is a color-term. The numerical preponderance of these four terms may therefore be due in part to their convenience as rime-words. How far this convenience influenced Chaucer in using a color rather than any other word we of course cannot say. Compare, in Fragment A of the *Romaunt*, the use of "grene" in rime in ll. 128, 731, 1581, where there is no word for green in the French.

As regards Chaucer's application of color, a reference to Table VII will show that more than one-half of it is expended by him in classes A, B, and C, that is, on Man, dress, and manufactured

articles used by men.   For as a colorist Chaucer is first and
foremost a portrait painter, studying not only the static color-
effects of the human face, but the dynamic changes effected in
the countenance by emotion.   See for example the passages *Tr.
and Cr.*, II, 645, 1198; III, 82; V, 243–5; *Anel.*, 353; *Duch.*, 497–9;
and in general his use of "asshen," "pale," and "wan;" his most
.notable picture of this sort is of course *Man of Law's Tale*, 645–
51.   In his studies of dress he is particularly exact and realistic,
especially as compared with a romantic poet like Spenser.   His
application of color to animals is made with genuine pleasure on
the poet's part, whether it be in a mere passing touch to a horse
(*Tr. and Cr.*, II, 624; *Kn. T.*, 2034; *Prol.*, 207), or in the elaborate
descriptions of the fox and the cock in the *Nonne Prestes Tale*.
From the birds of the *Parlement of Foules*, however, color is
notably absent; the goshawk is the only bird whose hue is mentioned.

When we turn from Man and the animal world to the field of
Nature, we find that the larger aspects of the landscape receive
very little study from Chaucer.   The cultivated field, the garden,
the well-kept meadow are his delight; he assigns no color to
mountains, and of his four color-adjectives applied to the sea,
" black " and " wan " are used with unpleasant significance (*Tr. and
Cr.*, II, 1, and *Kn. T.*, 1598), and "blue " and "green " occur quite
indefinitely of waves in *Kn. T.*, 1100, and *Former Age*, 21.   Flowers he certainly loved, and his especial worship of the daisy needs
no mention here.   In meadow, plant, and tree he notices but one
hue — green, and describes but one season — spring.   The month
of May, " moder of monthes glade," is his delight, and he chooses
its dawning life and starting foliage as the background for much
of his poetic narrative.   Allusion to the spring season is characteristic also of Gower, and still more of mediæval French poets,
but Chaucer's description of Maytime reveals to us a real and not
a conventional lover of the dawn of the year.

Compared with Langland and Gower, then, Chaucer has
advanced in the use of color in a marked degree.   He trebles
their vocabulary, he avoids their defects of range, he studies with
attentive realism the countenance and dress of human beings, he

paints a few lifelike pictures of animals, and he begins, with the opening year, that loving description of Nature which is to culminate four centuries later in the English Romantic School. His strength of course lies in his portrait-painting; and an example of his sensitive color-eye and his poetic taste in this respect may be seen in his treatment of Boccaccio's original in *Tr. and Cr.*, I, stanzas 25 and 26. (*Cf.* Ballerstedt, *loc. cit.*, pp. 55–6.) Boccaccio, speaking of the fair widowed Cressida among the other Trojan dames, compares her to a rose among violets; Chaucer, seeing Cressida before his mental eye, says there was never seen "under cloude blak so bright a sterre."

This single example may serve to show the definiteness and delicacy of Chaucer's color-pictures. Every quick, light touch of color which he lays on a portrait is made with insight and with skill; his mind's eye sees each change in the complexion of his heroes and heroines, just as he notes the slight smile or the dropped eyes. (*Prol.*, 119; *Friar's T.*, 148; *Tr. and Cr.*, II, 505; *Cl. T.*, 612–13.) In the keenness of his vision in this respect he is the lineal ancestor of Shakspere, who will far surpass him, however, in his careless mastery of color, and in his free coinage of suggestive metaphysical terms unknown to the older, simpler poet.

IV.

Spenser's color-vocabulary stands, in respect to numerical fullness, exactly midway between that of Chaucer and that of Shakspere (Table I). As compared with Chaucer's, however, it shows a greater advance than mere numbers would indicate, inasmuch as its terms are, with few exceptions—"castory," "watchet," "blunket,"[1]—those in use today: they are modern, and used without symbolic meaning, or at least with only such symbolism as we readily understand. The chief difference between Spenser's vocabulary and that of today lies in the compound rather than in the staple hues. Spenser and Shakspere made compounds by

---

[1] *Castory* is used as a synonym of vermilion (*F. Q.*, II, ix, 41). *Watchet* is a blue of varying shades (*F. Q.*, III, iv, 40: IV, xi, 17). *Blunket*, though usually a gray-blue, Spenser himself defines in his gloss as gray (*Shep. Cal.*, *May*, 5).

prefixing to the staple color-adjectives — *e. g.*, red and white — the name of some object or dye or material whose color was steady and therefore helped to make more definite the adjective itself. Good examples of such compounds are "rose-red," "snow-white," "fiery-red," "scarlet-red," "crimson-red," "lily-white," "milk-white," "grass-green." The Elizabethan poets almost never made tints and shades, as our later poets do, by means of the prefixes pale, light, dark, deep, etc. (pp. 111–12); Shakspere has no tints and but one shade —"deep-green" (*Complaint,* 213); Spenser has no shade and but two tints —"pallid-blue" (*Prothal.,* 30) and "pallid-green" (*Gnat,* 222).[1]

I have said that Spenser's vocabulary of color is modern, readily understood. It is also definite, so far as it can be cata-logued, with the single exception of the term "purple," most uncertain of all the hues used by English poets. One feels almost warranted in including Spenser's purple with his red, especially when it is used of blood, since the choice between the two seems one of rhythm and rime rather than of hue. (Compare, for example, *F. Q.,* I, ii, 14, 9, with I, ii, 17, 9 ; II, viii, 36, with II, viii, 37 ; III, i, 65, with III, vii, 17.)

In his color-scale (Table V) Spenser differs from other poets of his own and earlier time in lifting Yellows to a promi-nent place and subordinating Blacks. In this he was followed by Keats, with whom he agrees more closely than with any other of· the poets represented here. This preference on Spenser's part for yellow and dislike of black we may see not only in Table V, but also in IV, where "golden" appears as Spenser's most fre-quent color-word, and in III, where his percentage of Yellows is the largest, and that of Blacks next to the smallest, recorded. What Mr. Havelock Ellis says of Keats is true also of Spenser : "No great poet is more licentious in the use of 'golden' as a mere piece of poetic slang" (*loc. cit.,* p. 722).

Spenser's application of color shows that Man and problems connected with Man were of pre-eminent interest to him. In

[1] In these passages it is possible that pallid may mean dull or dark, thus forming a shade instead of a tint. Spenser probably had in mind such classical phrases as Virgil's "*pallentis violas*" and "*pallente hedera.*"

spite of his argument in *An Hymn in Honour of Beauty* that "that same goodly hew of white and red, with which the cheekes are sprinckled," and "those sweete rosy leaves, so fairely spred upon the lips," and "that golden wyre,"

shall fade and fall away
To that they were, even to corrupted clay,

he applies 58 per cent. of his color to man and his clothing, (Table VII), going not a whit beyond Chaucer in his percentage of Nature hues. Though he not infrequently notes, like Chaucer, that the human countenance is "ashy," "pale," "pallid," or "wan" because of emotion, his most distinctive touches are intended to indicate beauty. Take, for example, his Whites: here, in addition to the two ordinary terms "white" and "pale," and other terms of infrequent occurrence, he has "silver" 53 times, "snowy" 34, "hoary" 28, "ivory" 14, "lily" 12. He has developed what we might term the poetic Whites, at the expense of the standard word; but that he was led to do this by a discriminating perception of differing tones in the white objects described is much to be doubted. Probably exigencies of meter, or desire for alliteration, or the instinct for beauty and variety, decided whether he should call a woman'sskin "white," "snowy," "ivory," "alabaster," "marble," "silver," "cream," or "lily." His catalogues of a lovely woman's charms remind one of Gower, though they have less artificiality. (See, for example, *Amoretti*, XV and LXIV.)

Spenser's Nature painting is more varied than Chaucer's, but still scanty. He gives less color to all forms of Nature put together than to man's body, and for the greater aspects of the physical world — sky, plain, and sea — he has fewer pigments than for dress alone. For vegetation he has only the adjectives "green," "pallid-green," and "pallid;" for the ocean no realistic hues; for mountains none except "green" (*F. Q.*, I, vii, 32). He does, however, show a special fondness for silver streams, and he notices flowers with some minuteness and with apparent enjoyment—the "Pink and purple Columbine" (*Shep. Cal., April,* 136), "the violet, pallid blue" (*Prothalamion,* 30), "the purple hyacine"

(*Gnat*, 670), fleur-de-lis "with silken curtains and golden cover-
lets " (*F. Q.*, II, vi, 16), etc.

His best coloring in the larger Nature fields is given to the
sky, but even here he is decorative rather than discriminating;
and he usually places any passages descriptive of the hues of
clouds and heavens at the beginnings of cantos, where some new
action takes its rise (*F. Q.*, II, iii, 1 ; xi, 3). In this he seems to
follow afar those mediæval poets who determined by the position
of the planets and the season of the year the time of each event,
although in Spenser the astrology is omitted and only its accompanying romantic adornment remains.   The rainbow he thinks
"goodly," but he is content to speak of its hues in the most general terms, as in *F. Q.*, V, iii, 25.   Contrast with this bit of classic
conventionality Thomson's scientific list of spectrum hues (*Newton*, 96–118), or the description of the bow written by William
Browne, one of Spenser's own contemporaries — a description
crowded with homely yet true observation (*Britannia's Pastorals*,
II, 3).

Spenser constantly made natural scenery the background of
his romantic imaginings, and he enjoyed color ; but he did not
observe nice differences in Nature's hues.   Indeed, before Milton
no English poet of the first rank looked upon Nature as other
than the stage of human action.   Perhaps we could not expect
the poetic-realistic landscape to appear in literature in an age
when the landscape backgrounds on the painter's canvas were so
eminently stiff in outline and crude in coloring as were those of
Italy in Spenser's day.

In frequency of color-usage Spenser is considerably in
advance of Chaucer ; and yet, after studying all of the hues
which his verse yields to the cataloguer, one remains unsatisfied.
Why is it, we ask ourselves, that we carry from the reading of
Spenser an impression of so much brightness and color when he
averages (Table II) but 17 color-terms per 1,000 lines?

Let us go again to his verse for an answer to this question.
We shall find there something which eludes the cataloguer,
but which, nevertheless, has its influence upon the reader — a
constant color-hinting that, in conjunction with the reader's

imagination, contributes a brilliant gorgeousness or a dire gloom to his pages. (See *F. Q.*, III, xi, 47; V, iii, 25; *Gnat*, 97–120; *Muiopotmos*, 330–5.)   In addition to the more specific terms, Spenser has hosts of nondescripts : "divers colourd," "sundry colourd," "painted," "discolourd" (= diverse), "perfect hue," "lovely hue," "goodly hue," "likely hue," "manly hue," "uncouth hue," "horrible hue," "loathsome hue," "hellish hue," "crabbed hue," "hated hue," "deadly hue," "filthy hue," "angels hue," "celestial hue," "heavenly hue," "orient hue," "heartless hollow hue."   Nowhere, unless perhaps in Swinburne's verse, is the color-idea so ever-present and yet so evasive.   And when we add to this poet's glowing Golds the constantly hinted glitter and sheen of much of his verse, we understand why Spenser seems to us a rich colorist, the forerunner of Keats.

V.

With Milton color-emphasis shifts from Man to Nature.   To sky, landscape, and waters he applies 47 per cent. of his color, as contrasted with Spenser's 18 per cent. and Shakspere's 13 per cent.   In his flower and fruit hues, also, he is relatively strong (Table VII).   The proportion in which he uses the different color-groups, moreover, shows his study of Nature : he has less red and white—the human colors *par excellence* — but more green, blue, and gray than his predecessors (Table III).

Milton's vocabulary is not large in the line of color (p. 105). It contains fewer terms than Chaucer used, fewer than Pope or Cowper used ; and none of its terms need special comment, if we understand that "blank" (*P. L.*, X, 656) means white, and that "grain"[1] means one of the hues made with cochineal dye.   Nor is he lavish in using this vocabulary, for he rises but one word above Chaucer in his average per 1,000 lines (Table II).

Yet it may be said of Milton that, though he used color spar-

---

[1] For a full discussion of *grain* as used by Milton see G. P. Marsh : *Lectures on the English Language*, Lecture III (Scribner, 1859).

Spenser used *grain* to mean, not the crimson or purple dye, but a fast dye of any hue, as in *Shep. Cal.*, *Feb.*, 132.

ingly, he was everywhere master of it.   He was never beguiled
into adorning his verse with it from mere poetic habit.   In
almost every instance where hue occurs in his verse it is used
with artistic effect, whether it be the dark and baleful shades that
render more hideous hell and its foul denizens, or the bright
illuminated colors that curtain the sun at dawn, or prank the
meadows, or mantle with regal ornament angel and archangel.

The colors in his verse are distinctly beautiful.   They are
kept pure.   They are never degraded by association with
unpleasant objects.   In these respects he forms the strongest of
contrasts with Pope (see pp. 17–21).   To the student of Milton
the mere mention of color-words, selected at random, will call up
a train of exquisite imagery—for example, "amber" (*L'Allegro,*
61); "blue" (*Lycidas,* 192); "carnation" (*P. L.,* IX., 429); "dun"
(*P. L.,* III, 72); [1] "gold" (*P. L.,* V, 277–87); "gray" (*P. L.,* IV,
598; V, 186–8; *Lycidas,* 187); "green" (*Comus,* 232; *P. L.,* VII,
316; *Lycidas,* 140); "pale," "wan," or "jet" (*Lycidas,* 139–48);
"purple" (*P. L.,* VII, 30); "red" (*P. L.,* VIII, 619; *Nativity,* 230);
"rosy" (*P. L.,* V, 1); "russet" (*L'Allegro,* 71); "sable" (*Il
Penseroso,* 35); "sapphire" (*Music,* 7); "silver" (*Arcades,* 14–16);
"white" (*Samson,* 327; *Comus,* 213; *P. L.,* XI, 206).   These
passages alone are sufficient to prove the delicacy and the
dignity of Milton's coloring.   With single, clear, artistic
touches of color he adds beauty to pictures whose main effects
are attained by other means.   He nowhere masses his hues, but
whenever he touches them he shows a masterly skill in their
handling and a refined appreciation of their real and ideal
beauty.

In the works of the majority of poets light and shade are
found to play a larger part than defined hues.   This I have
mentioned in connection with Spenser, and shall have occasion
to emphasize in treating the color of Wordsworth and Keats.
But of no one is it more true than of him who, out of his "ever-
during dark," cried—

> Hail, holy Light ! offspring of Heaven firstborn !
> Or of the Eternal coëternal beam

[1] Contrast Pope's one use of "dun," *Dunciad,* II, 38.

> May I express thee unblamed? since God is light
> And never but in unapproached light
> Dwelt from eternity—dwelt then in thee,
> Bright effluence of bright essence increate.
> —*P. L.*, III, 1–6.

Did Milton's blindness increase his joy in "the sovereign vital lamp," as he in memory revisited its realms? And did it affect his choice of colors or his manner of using them? These questions it is interesting to attempt to answer, even though we reach no ·indisputable conclusions. If we compute separately the color-usages of the poems written before 1654—the date of Milton's blindness—and those written after this date, we find that he was about four times more lavish of color in the earlier poems than in the later. In accounting for this we must consider, first, that poets in general use more color in youth than in maturity; second, that there is an essential difference between the themes of Milton's two periods, the pastoral, descriptive character of *Lycidas*, *Comus*, *L'Allegro*, and *Il Penseroso* inviting a larger amount of color than one would expect in epics of lofty and didactic purpose, like the *Paradise Lost*, or in classical dramas like *Samson Agonistes*. Yet, in addition to these two influential factors in the lessening of Milton's definite color and the increase of glooms and glories, which we note in his great epics and the *Samson*, I think that we may detect a third influence, which helps to make the color-scale of the *Paradise Lost* run from dusk to gold and radiant white, rather than through spectrum hues, and which also leads the poet to select his few bright hues for their richness and distinctness—"red," "purple," "azure," "amber," "gold;"—and this influence was the extinction, for him, of

> Light, the prime work of God.
> —*Samson*, 70.

CHAPTER II.

POPE'S USE OF COLOR.

Text used : *Poetical Works.* Globe edition. Macmillan, 1889.
Number of lines, 10,287.
For vocabulary see p. 106.

We are accustomed to see in Pope the typical " Classicist," to regard him as the master, in English verse, of terse, polished dialectics, of bitter satire, of brilliant conventionalities. And therefore we turn to his verse expecting to find in it little or no color. The *Essay on Man,* or the *Essay on Criticism,* or the *Dunciad* would seem to create as little opportunity for color as did *Piers the Plowman.*

Unexpectedly, however, the sum of Pope's color proves by no means insignificant. In his 10,287 lines of verse color-terms occur 297 times, averaging 29 words per 1,000 lines, a proportion greater than that of Coleridge or Wordsworth or Byron, double that of Chaucer or Milton, and two and one-half times that of Shakspere (Table II). In his relative proportions of different hues Pope most nearly resembles Keats (Table III); and in range of application he is so symmetrical that his color is given about equally to Man and to Nature (Table VII).

We cannot help challenging such results as these which the tables furnish. We cannot help asking if it be possible that these data, indicating a fuller color-perception than that of the great Romanticists, correctly represent the polished epigrammatist and caustic wit of the eighteenth century.

A little study of Pope's color-passages will show that, although the average of his work as a whole indicates equal attention on his part to Man and to Nature, no single important poem betrays such symmetry. All of his Nature coloring worthy of mention — hues of flowers and foliage, of field and sky, of birds and fishes — is massed in four or five poems which have the slightest

14

possible allusion to human coloring, and these poems are his earliest.

Pope's work is divisible into two distinct parts. In the first fall the poems of his boyhood, *Windsor Forest*[1] and the four *Pastorals*, which were written, according to the poet's own testimony, before he was seventeen ; in the second falls the remainder of his verse, composed mainly after he had joined himself to the wits of the

Dear, damn'd, distracting town.

I have said that his poetry is divisible. One may go further and say that a division must necessarily be made in order to obtain a just notion of Pope as a colorist. Stating the figures at once, in the 820 lines of his five early poems 65 per cent. of the color-vocabulary is bright ; the color-average per 1,000 lines is 85 words, a total higher than that of any poet here catalogued ; and 90 per cent. of this color is applied to Nature. But the remainder of his poetic work, 9,467 lines, has an average of 24 words of color per 1,000 lines, applies but 34 per cent. of these to Nature, and uses a vocabulary more than half of whose terms are Neutrals and Browns. It will be seen that in his youth, when under the influence of Latin authors and of a suburban environment, Pope started out to be a Nature poet, and set his palette with bright embellishing colors that would help to create the illusion deemed by him the proper atmosphere for the pastoral, colors that would present to his readers "the most agreeable objects of the country," that would furnish "beautiful digressions," that were, in short, like his shepherds, not so truly what he saw about him at Binfield or Windsor Forest as what he might conceive to have been there in the golden age.[2] Virgil, whose verse is full of glow and color, was Pope's chosen model among pastoral poets.

The coloring in Pope's *Pastorals* may be summed up under the epithet "agreeable." It is not far removed from reality, but it

[1] The latter part of *Windsor Forest* was added shortly before publication in 1713, but the descriptions of Nature were written in 1704, according to Pope's own note on the poem, as cited below.

[2] See Pope's *Discourse on Pastoral Poetry.*

does not bear the indubitable stamp of first-hand observation ; it has upon it, rather, the glamour of the golden age. The blue violet "glows," "blushing berries paint the yellow grove," swans are "silver," honey is a "golden store," the bull and turtle-dove brought for sacrifice are "milk-white," dew is "rosy,"[1] flocks eat their "verdant food" on the banks of "silver Thame," and "lavish Nature paints the purple year." There are, too, some color-touches of real, if rather conventional, beauty : the "whitening vale" of morning, the dawn "blushing on the mountain side," and the "groves that shine with silver frost."

In the *Windsor Forest* we come still nearer to the actual hues of Nature. We feel that the poet had had his eye upon the object before he wrote —

> Here in full light the russet plains extend :
> There wrapt in clouds the bluish hills ascend.
> Ev'n the wild heath displays her purple dyes,

although immediately after this bit of realistic beauty he falls again into the use of a stereotyped phraseology, in which trees

> Like verdant isles the sable waste adorn,

and

> . . . . blushing Flora paints th' enamelled ground.

The lines of this poem in which he describes the hunted pheasant and "the scaly breed " sought by the angler are worthy of quotation as containing the most brilliant coloring to be found anywhere in Pope's work :

> See ! from the brake the whirring pheasant springs,
> And mounts exulting on triumphant wings :
> Short is his joy ; he feels the fiery wound,
> Flutters in blood, and panting beats the ground.
> Ah ! what avail his glossy, varying dyes,
> His purple crest, and scarlet-circled eyes,
> The vivid green his shining plumes unfold,
> His painted wings, and breast that flames with gold ?
>   —*W. F.*, 111–18.

[1] "Rosy " is evidently used here to convey a pleasing general impression, not a color. The word "purple " in the "purple year " (*Sp.*, 28) is likewise used of vivid color in general, not of a distinct hue. See Warburton's note on this line.

Our plenteous streams a various race supply,
The bright-eyed perch with fins of Tyrian dye,
The silver eel, in shining volumes roll'd,
The yellow carp, in scales bedropp'd with gold,
Swift trouts, diversified with crimson stains,
And pikes, the tyrants of the wat'ry plains.
— *W. F.*, 141–6.

One would like to know just how much Pope altered the
Windsor Forest between its composition in 1704 and its publication in 1713. We know from his own note[1] that the historical
and political allusions of the latter part (beginning probably with
line 290) were written last. The opening lines, too, must have
been rewritten, that they might show the name of Granville, to
whom the poem was dedicated when published. And to one
acquainted with Pope's habit of changing his former utterances,
and concealing such change where possible, it would seem no
strange thing if he altered the earlier part of the *Windsor Forest*
without mentioning the fact. If one had the exact facts before
him, it would be interesting to see if Pope's decision to be a
painter, reached in 1712, made him more sensitive to color at
that time than he had been before. He did actually study for
eighteen months under a pupil of the portrait-painter Kneller,
at this period of his life, but we know little more of the result of
that study than that he threw away, when he returned to literature, "three Dr. Swifts, two Lady Bridgewaters, a Duchess of
Montague, half a dozen earls, and one knight of the garter."

It is, perhaps, as well that he did throw away his gallery of
portraits, if eighteenth-century society was to be presented there in
hues as disagreeable as those with which its members are depicted
in his verse. For, turning to the second division of his work,
that in which Man receives the greater proportion of his coloring, we shall find that after his early pastoral poems Pope abandoned almost entirely the use of color as an embellishment. He
still handled hues, but not that he might present to his readers

---

[1] "This poem was written at two different times: the first part of it, which
relates to the country, in the year 1704, at the same time with the Pastorals; the
latter part was not added till the year 1715, in which it was published."—*P.*

agreeable images. They were now abusive epithets, the instruments of his satire. His color-vocabulary is increased by words like "sallow," "adust," "brown," "black-and-blue," "livid," "gray," "black," "dun," "dusky," and "swarthy," all of which were unpleasant to him, and of his earlier colors there is scarcely one that he does not degrade by associating it with the artificial or the loathsome. Take, as an example of this degrading of colors, the passages where "yellow" occurs. They are six in number, three in his early, three in his later poems. This color was certainly used to add beauty in the lines —

> Now blushing berries paint the yellow grove.
> —*Autumn*, 75.

> O'er sandy wilds were yellow harvests spread.
> —*W. F.*, 88.

> The yellow carp, in scales bedropped with gold.
> —*W. F.*, 144.

But how unpleasant are the images called up here ! —

> All seems infected that th' infected spy,
> As all looks yellow to the jaundiced eye.
> —*Es. Crit.*, 558–9.

> Is yellow dirt the passion of thy life ?
> —*Es. Man*, IV, 279.

> On once a flock-bed, but repaired with straw,
> With tape-ty'd curtains, never meant to draw,
> The George and Garter dangling from that bed
> Where tawdry yellow strove with dirty red,
> Great Villiers lies ! . . . .
> —*Mor. Es.*, III, 301–5.

The last quotations are typical of all of Pope's later poetry, so far as it deals with color. Its subjects were such as to afford small opportunity for descriptions of external Nature, and of the beauties of human color Pope seems to have had slight appreciation. Perhaps his own bodily weakness and deformity made him disregard, through jealousy, the splendid vigor or delicate beauty of others.

Pope's portraits are those of the etcher, in the main. Only now and then does he give them a touch of color, and when he does it is the merest touch. We find one mention of blue eyes (*Moral Essays*, II, 284), but it is mechanical. It has behind it neither the frank appreciation of beauty that prompted Scott's "eye of matchless blue," nor the emotion that moved Keats to write of eyes whose blue runs liquid through the soul. The shade of hair appealed so little to Pope that he could write four cantos of *The Rape of the Lock* before mentioning the hue of the reft curl, and then be content with a single stroke of color (*Rape*, IV, 169). Red hair is once referred to (*Gulliver*, IV, 27), and gray hair three times (*Rape*, V, 28; *Moral Essays*, III, 327; *Dunciad*, III, 103). Otherwise the hue of hair is unnoticed.

We next ask how Pope treats what Spenser calls

> that same goodly hew of white and red
> With which the cheekes are sprinckled.

His favorite word for suggesting color in the face is "blush," but it is the blush of shame or of the rouge box, not that of modesty or beauty. The "nymph" who performs at the cosmetic table the "sacred rites of Pride"

> Repairs her smiles, awakens every grace,
> And calls forth all the wonders of her face;
> Sees by degrees a purer blush arise,
> And keener lightenings kindle in her eyes.
> —*Rape*, I, 141-4.

Ariel bids the sylphs who attend the fair nymphs to

> Assist their blushes and inspire their airs.
> —*Rape*, II, 98.

If we question Pope's other Reds in the hope that they will prove less artificial, we are doomed to disappointment. The term "red" itself he applies three times to the face, in the following passages:

> But Appius reddens at each word you speak.
> — *Es. Crit.*, 585.

> She was my friend; I taught her first to spread
> Upon her sallow cheeks enlivening red.
> —*Basset-Table*, 101-2.

> No! let a charming chintz, and Brussels lace
> Wrap my cold limbs, and shade my lifeless face :
> One would not, sure, be frightful when one 's dead —
> And — Betty — give this Cheek a little Red.
>
> *—Mor. Es.*, I, 248–51.

Even "rose" has the scent of the toilet table with its "Puffs, Powders, Patches, Bibles, Billet-doux," in the lines —

> There Affectation with a sickly mien
> Shows in her cheeks the roses of eighteen.
>
> (*Rape*, IV, 31–2),

although it is real, for once, when Eloisa says :

> See from my cheeks the transient roses fly.
>
> *—Eloisa*, 331.

The few citations above, with a single mention of "ruby lips" (*Elegy on an Unfortunate Lady*, 31), bring before us every instance of Pope's use of warm or bright colors in depicting men and women, excepting his rather frequent "blush." How thoroughly artificial his treatment is here, and how far removed from any attempt to render mankind beautiful, is evident at a glance. As I have already remarked, color became, in the hands of the flattered wit of London literary circles, merely an instrument of satire. He no longer strove, as he had striven in the *Pastorals*, to render his subject "extremely sweet and pleasing." His object was now to chronicle the disagreeable rather than the agreeable, and he therefore chooses hues which are not decorative but dirty and tawdry. He does make polite mention of Belinda's white breast and snowy neck, but elsewhere he remarks upon the color of skin only to condemn it as ugly. Henley stands in the *Dunciad* "embrowned in native bronze." Lintot's face shows "brown dishonours." We read of the mud-nymphs "Nigrina black and Merdamante brown" as vying for the love of an archbishop "in jetty bowers below," and of this same prelate as surrounded by "a sable army," a "black troop,"

> A low-born, cell-bred, selfish, servile band,
> Prompt or to guard or stab, to saint or damn.

Complexions are "adust," " sable," " swarthy," "pale," or over·
spread with "livid paleness."

But why should we quote farther? It would only lead to
such revolting pictures as that of Obloquy with

> Mouth as black as bull-dogs at the stall
>
> (*Imit. Spens.*, 38),

or of the

> muse-rid mope, adust and thin,
> In a dun nightgown of his own loose skin.
>
> —*Dunciad*, II, 37–8.

We may drop here the consideration of Pope's color-treatment of Man with the remark that, just as the coloring of
Nature in his *Pastorals* can be summed up under the epithet
"agreeable," so the coloring given to Man in his later and chief
period may be summed up under the epithet "disagreeable."

In conclusion, then, we find that Pope passed through two distinct phases as a colorist. In his youth colors appealed to him as
beautifying, if not distinctly beautiful, and he used them freely to
adorn his verse. At this period he chose warm or vivid hues, and
he applied them wholly to Nature. Though in the main he echoed
color-uses of the Latin and English poets whom he admired,[1] in
a few cases, such as his mention of "bluish hills" and of the
heather's "purple dyes," he was probably recording independent
observations. Had he lived in the country, apart from the influ-
ences of the London literary life which in his day lent its heartiest
appreciation to neatly expressed moral sentiments and stinging
invective, Pope might perhaps have been a Nature poet. But his
first publications won for him immediate notice, and by the
time he was nineteen he was launched into London society and
carried along in the tide of prevailing literary opinion. His
ready wit was discovered and complimented, and he entirely
abandoned his earlier tendencies to pastoral verse.

In this complete change in Pope's ideals we have that which
accounts for the apparently symmetrical color-interest shown in

[1] See the notes to the *Pastorals* and *Windsor Forest*, in the Elwell and
Courthope edition of Pope's works.

Table VII—as toward Man and Nature—and it is this change which finally stamps him a Classicist of the Classicists rather than a forerunner of the Romanticists. Further, it is the formal, conventional application of his numerically abundant color that debars him from taking rank as a genuine student of Nature, and that accounts for the seeming paradoxes of Tables I, II, III, VII. Pope's 29 color-terms as against Wordsworth's 22, and his 47 per cent. of color given to Nature as compared with Keats's 54 per cent., are inconsistencies fully accounted for when we have studied his color-terms in their contexts.

CHAPTER III.

THOMSON'S USE OF COLOR.

Text used : *Poetical Works*. Aldine edition. 2 vols. Bell & Daldy, 1867.
Number of lines, 13,158.
For vocabulary see p. 106.

When the eighteenth century entered upon its second quarter
in England, Alexander Pope was indisputably the foremost living
poet, critic, and translator. His poetic work both in manner and
matter became the model for the literary productions of his day.
But just at this time appeared the first publication of a poet who,
while admiring and honoring Pope, was to point the way along
paths widely divergent from the straight highroad of the Classicists. This publication was James Thomson's *Winter*, issued
in 1726.

It is not necessary here to enumerate and explain the many
ways in which Thomson foreshadowed the school of poets which
ushered in the next century. It is of Thomson as a colorist that
we have to speak, though even when we confine ourselves to this
one aspect of his work, we shall find that he represents here, in
little, the return to nature, the appreciation of the specific as well
as the general, and the valuation of the commonplace and the
humble as well as of the ideal and the noble — all of which are
characteristics of the coming Romantic age.

Thomson's reputation is generally acknowledged to rest upon
the *Seasons* and the *Castle of Indolence*. If to these we add the
lines *To the Memory of Sir Isaac Newton*, we have named all of
his work that is of interest to the student of color. In bulk, these
poems constitute 7,028 of his 13,158 lines,[1] and in color-words
they are more than twice as rich as the remainder of his verse.[2]

[1] Dramas not included.

[2] They average 52 color-words per 1,000 lines, as opposed to an average of
21 in the rest of his work.

23

The data given in the following pages are, however, drawn from his work as a whole, with the exception of the dramas.

Perhaps there is no quicker way to reach an appreciation of this poet's coloring than to compare his *Winter* with earlier poems on the same subject. By such a comparison Thomson is at once revealed as the observer of Nature, as the man who relies for his colors upon his memory of the real thing, rather than upon an established poetical vocabulary or upon an imagination trained along the lines of the classic pastoral.

For examples of earlier poems on winter, take Spenser's *January* and *December*, in the *Shepherd's Calendar*, and Pope's fourth *Pastoral*.

Colin Clout observes no coloring in the January landscape but the "pale and wan" face of the shepherd and the "hoary frost" on the naked trees, whose shady leaves are lost and whose sorrowful tears depend in dreary icicles from their boughs. In December, Colin's own head being now besprent with "hoary frost," he moans to Pan,

> hearken a while, from your green cabinet.

These are all of Spenser's winter color-touches. There is no indication here of an enjoyment of the season, or of attention to any features of it but its cold and desolation.

Pope's *Winter* has but one line of characteristic winter coloring—

> Behold the groves that shine with silver frost,

which might seem to express real appreciation of the season's beauties, were it not followed by

> Their beauty withered, and their verdure lost.

The remaining color-touches of the poem are mere bits of gilding taken from the conventional pastoral palette: "silver swans," "silver flood," "golden store" of honey, and imagined "groves for ever green."

But in Thomson's *Winter* the colors used, though open to the charge of being commonplace, are the outcome of real observation, made with real interest. Take the passage where the poet is describing the decline of a day in early winter, when a tem-

pestuous storm is gathering. The "weak, wan" sun skirts the
southern sky, while the "deep-tinged" clouds involve in "sable"
shadows the furrowed land where crop the "dun discolour'd
flocks." Then comes forth the tempest "wrapped in black
glooms," and soon

> Th' unsightly plain
> Lies a brown deluge; as the low bent clouds
> Pour flood on flood, yet unexhausted still
> Combine, and deepening into night, shut up
> The day's fair face
>
> * * * * * * * *
>
> When from the pallid sky the sun descends,
> With many a spot that o'er his glaring orb
> Uncertain wanders, stain'd; red, fiery streaks
> Begin to flush around. The reeling clouds
> Stagger with dizzy poise, as doubting yet
> Which master to obey; while rising slow,
> Blank, in the leaden-colour'd east, the moon
> Wears a wan circle round her blunted horns.
> Seen through the turbid, fluctuating air,
> The stars obtuse emit a shiver'd ray;
> Or frequent seem to shoot athwart the gloom,
> And long behind them trail the whitening blaze.
>
> —*Winter*, 76-129.

Then "the black night . . . . sits immense around," and
the "weary clouds . . . . mingle into solid gloom." But with
the morning "Through the hushed air the whitening shower
descends," and the fields "Put on their winter robe of purest
white."

Here we have a series of pictures sketched in the main in
Blacks and Whites. But the poet goes farther and sees, besides the
predominant hues, others quite as true to the winter landscape.
He sees the "brown inhabitants" of the wilds (257), the "blue
serene of the frosty sky" (693), the "blue crust of ice" that
glazes over the "marbled snow" (858), the "azure gloss" on icy
mountains (783), the "drooping roses" of a wintry east (947),
the "transient hues" of fair frostwork; or the "blue film" that the
icy gale breathes over the pool (724).

Every tint here is evidence of the poet's quick eye and loving memory for Nature's winter moods, in treating which as subjects for verse he was breaking ground in a new poetic field. And inasmuch as the field of observation was new, it is not surprising that he developed here some methods of working peculiarly his own—methods which he continued to employ in his later productions.

In his work as a whole, but especially in the *Seasons*, Thomson displays some distinct mannerisms in his conception and treatment of

All this innumerous-colour'd scene of things.
                                                —Spring, 568.

These I mention below, with illustrative references :

(*a*) A careful discrimination between tints differing from one another as slightly as these of the "blank" moon, its "wan circle," and the "leaden-colour'd east." This tendency to the study of relative values is very characteristic of Thomson, and finds expression in various ways: in the description of the gradation of hues shown in a group of objects; in a fondness for studying the transition from shade to shade in a single object ; and in a preference for the comparative degree of the color-adjective to the neglect of the superlative, a preference which seems to accord with that general dislike, on Thomson's part, of putting limits to his ideas which Dr. Reynolds calls his "dislike of boundaries" (*loc. cit.*, p. 82).

(*Spring*, 1047–8 ; *Summer*, 594–8; 1314–16 ; *Autumn*, 950–54.)

(*b*) A conception of color as living and moving. This leads Thomson to the frequent use of color-verbs—whiten, green, blush, flush, etc.— and to the still more frequent use of what we may call inchoative color-terms—whitening, reddening, etc. Like effects are also secured by such adjective modifiers of color-nouns as live, ardent, flaming, glowing, kindling. In this conception of color as in motion Thomson is a forerunner of Shelley.

(*Spring*, 320–21, 378, 961–4 ; *Summer*, 82–4, 1112, 1584–6 ; *Autumn*, 619, 1257–60; *Hymn*, 95–7 ; *Castle*, II, xxxv; *Liberty*, I, 160.)

(*c*) A fondness for colors due to moisture, manifesting itself in Thomson's interest in protoplastic movement as color-producing, and in his frequent descriptions of the hues of sky and vegetation during and after storms. (See references under (*d*).)

(*a*) Very frequent reference to abundant color without specification of hues. Here Thomson is like Spenser.

(*Spring*, 79–83, 184–97, 551, 561–8.)

(*e*) A delight in color for its own sake, to be seen especially in the poetic analysis of spectrum and rainbow hues.

(*Newton*, 96–118; *Summer*, 147–56; *Spring*, 526–35.)

The last three passages are, each in its own way, catalogues of the primary colors. They are, however, almost the only selections that one could make from Thomson's verse where more than two bright colors are mentioned together. We have, indeed, several tones of one color brought together frequently, as I have before mentioned; but there is seldom an expressed color-combination involving three or more primary hues.

Mr. William Hand Browne, in a brief article in *Modern Language Notes* for May, 1897, gives a list of "color-chords" that he has found in the *Seasons*. To the reader who does not seek out the passages on which Mr. Browne bases his statements the statements are decidedly misleading; for, instead of confining himself to the colors Thomson mentions (and the only colors we may legitimately assume he at the moment saw), Mr. Browne fills out the "chords" by naming the colors which the lines suggest to himself. Thus he gives as one of Thomson's chords "Green, white, and pink—fresh-sprung grass and hawthorn blossoms," which he evidently derives (though he nowhere gives references) from the lines :

> From the moist meadow to the wither'd hill,
> Led by the breeze, the vivid verdure runs,
> And swells and deepens to the cherish'd eye.
> The hawthorn whitens, ...
> —*Spring*, 87–90.

But, "pink" not being mentioned here, what right have we to assume that it was present in the poet's mind ? And, besides, Thomson nowhere uses the word "pink" for color.

Again Mr. Browne finds, apparently in the lines below, the chord "White, yellow, and purple":

> Where scattered wild the lily of the vale
> Its balmy essence breathes, where cowslips hang
> The dewy head, where purple violets lurk.

But, when it is the *fragrance* of the lily of the vale, and the *droop* of the cowslips that the poet expressly mentions, what reason have we to ascribe to him a color-chord based on hues which he has left unmentioned? In my opinion we have none.

To return to Thomson himself, the passages referred to above will show that, even though Thomson was often a but half-hatched Romanticist in his turning of phrases, he was a full-fledged Nature student as far as eye and heart were concerned. And they will show that he loved colors, the colors of natural objects just as he saw them before him, and that he took a scientist's delight in this teeming earth

> arrayed
> In all the colours of the flushing year.
>
> —*Spring*, 95.

In fact, color was for him one of Nature's chief delights. When night shut down, the earth lost for him all of its beauty:

> Sunk in the quenching Gloom,
> Magnificent and vast, are heaven and earth.
> Order confounded lies; all beauty void,
> Distinction lost, and gay variety
> One universal blot: such the fair Power
> Of light, to kindle and create the whole.
>
> —*Autumn*, 1139-44.

From his characterization of the various hues, one may guess which were most beautiful to him — not red, although that is the one which he oftenest associates with life and transition, but "gay green" (*Spring*, 82) and "delicious yellow" (*Newton*, 104) and "the pure blue that swells autumnal skies" (*Newton*, 106).

Of brown he has an unusually large percentage (Table III), even the fronds of a withered fern taking on to his eye a "friendly hue," but the reader does not feel that this was one of his colors of preference.

His feeling for green is the one oftenest expressed — notably in *Spring*, 82–5, where he speaks of

> Various hues, but chiefly thee, gay green!
> Thou smiling Nature's universal robe!
> United light and shade! where the sight dwells
> With growing strength and ever-new delight.

In this expressed delight in green, Thomson forms a link between Chaucer and Keats.

His chosen Blues are usually suggestive of repose, forming a marked contrast to his Reds. They are to him "gentle" (*Myra*, 3) and "pure" (*Newton*, 106).

A study of his Yellows will show that the majority of them are descriptive of the time of year dearest to him,[1]

> When Autumn's yellow lustre gilds the world.
> —*Autumn*, 1320.

The mention of Thomson's favorite hues, and especially of yellow as one, leads us to consider here the views of Mr. Havelock Ellis on this subject. In an article in the *Contemporary Review* for May, 1896, entitled "Color-Sense in Literature," Mr. Ellis has included in his generalizations certain remarks on Thomson as a colorist, in which he incidentally points out what he calls the poet's "colors of predilection." In his notes on the *Castle of Indolence* he says : "black here prevails enormously over white, and yellow is totally absent. The prominence of brown is remarkable." These statements are correct enough for the *Castle of Indolence*, a poem of 1,404 lines, constituting, if we omit from consideration the dramas, about one-ninth of the bulk of Thomson's work, but they do not warrant Mr. Ellis in constructing on this basis percentages which he places beside those drawn for example from "nearly the whole of [Coleridge's] poetic work"—20,000 lines in all—and in deducing, from this and other comparisons, general remarks as to the color-tendencies in English literature. As a matter of fact, an examination of 13,000 lines of Thomson's verse shows that he uses as many yellow tones as does Spenser or Keats, and that he had a marked

[1] Letter to Mr. Lyttleton, July, 1743.

personal fondness for the word yellow, preferring it, for example, to the term gold. In his use of the simple color-word he
passes any other English poet here catalogued ; and he even
speaks of it in his poem to Newton as "delicious yellow."

With regard to the "increasing prevalence of green" in
Thomson, as noted by Mr. Ellis, there is again an alteration
necessary in Mr. Ellis's generalizations, if we treat Thomson's
work as a whole. Comparing Thomson with Shakspere and
with Chaucer (Marlowe, who is included by Mr. Ellis, is not here
studied), we see that Mr. Ellis has put down for Shakspere
(*Sonnets* and *Venus and Adonis*) 9 per cent. of green, and for
Chaucer ("portions of the *Legend of Good Women* and the
Canterbury Tales") 14 per cent. of green. We pass without
comment the inexactitude of the Chaucerian references. Reck-
oning Thomson's use of green in the *Castle of Indolence* at
27 per cent., Mr. Ellis notes accordingly the increase there shown
in the use of this word, over preceding poets. The percentages,
however, drawn from the entire body of work of Chaucer, Shakspere, and Thomson show for the *word* green : Chaucer, 21 per
cent. ; Shakspere, 13 per cent. ; Thomson, 18 per cent. There is,
of course, an increase in Thomson's work as compared with that
of Shakspere, though not so great an increase as Mr. Ellis's 27
per cent. for Thomson would indicate ; but Thomson is rather
behind the fourteenth-century poet Chaucer in the frequency of
green. If we consider, however, the Greens as a group, and
include verdant and other variants of the simple color, we have
results as shown in Table III appended to this essay. The data
immediately preceding have been made on Mr. Ellis's plan to
admit of exact comparison.

Take, next, Mr. Ellis's statement that "black here prevails enormously over white," with his percentages 36 and 9, deduced from
2 uses of white and 8 of black in the *Castle of Indolence*, a poem
which, as before stated, constitutes one-ninth of Thomson's work.
In the remaining eight-ninths of Thomson's work, however, we find
just 40 uses of the word "white" and 40 uses of the word "black ;"
it is, therefore, only in the one poem selected by Mr. Ellis for
examination that Thomson happens to use more black than

white. This is unfortunate for Mr. Ellis's generalization, which apparently is that, though Thomson was liberal of black, and Blake " had a distinct predilection for it," Coleridge brought in " a return to white and corresponding repugnance to black, which has ever since characterized English literature." (In this connection we may remark that black is decidedly Byron's color of predilection and is in Coleridge himself only second to green, and therefore more frequent than white.) It is true that both Thomson and Coleridge associate black as a color with unpleasant images —Thomson uses it almost entirely for gloomy personifications, and for storm hues —and it is also true that Coleridge has more uses of the word white than Thomson, Gray, or Cowper, though much less than Scott; but the numerical facts, drawn out on the same plan as that followed in Mr. Ellis's tables, are as below stated. Numbering the uses of the words black and white, in the poets above named, we find them as follows : Thomson, 48 and 42; Gray, 3 and 3; Cowper, 12 and 10; Scott, 56 and 87; Coleridge, 57 and 55; Wordsworth, 63 and 122. Scott or Wordsworth, rather than Coleridge, would therefore be the bringer-back of white into English literature, if we choose to consider such a thing as possible; as a matter of fact, however, taking the Whites as a group, and stating the percentage of usage, we find that this color-group has remained more constant throughout English literature than has any other (Table III), forming from one-fourth to one-third of the color-effect of almost every great poet from Langland to Keats.

Finally, with regard to Thomson's colors of predilection, Mr. Ellis defines this phrase "of predilection" to mean "used with special frequency as compared with other writers" (*loc. cit.*, p. 717), and he then states Thomson's as brown, black, and green. As a matter of fact, the evidence of Thomson's entire work, adapted to Mr. Ellis's standpoint, shows that they are black, blue, and red. " Predominant " colors —still following Mr. Ellis's method —are in Thomson, as a whole, red and black. Mr. Ellis gives black and green. Classing the colors into groups, on the lines here laid down, and including with each main color-word all of its synonyms, we find that in Thomson's verse the groups which lead

numerically are Whites, Reds, and Greens — the same trio which
Chaucer and Wordsworth place first in their verse.

That Thomson is a forerunner of the Romanticists is evident
to one who studies his color; but it is well to note in this connection that his percentages of color-distribution show that he is
such a forerunner on the Nature side only.   The Romanticists
are characterized by a fullness of color-interest — an interest which
embraces both Man and Nature.   The interest in Man had already
been shown to a marked degree in the color-vocabulary and color-
distribution of the Elizabethans.   The interest in Nature had,
however, no marked exponent before Thomson; but in him it so
outstripped the human interest that as a colorist he stands, among
the poets here studied, as the extreme Nature type.

CHAPTER IV.

I. GRAY'S USE OF COLOR.

Text used: *Works*, Vol. I. Gosse's edition. 4 vols. Worthington, 1854.
Number of lines, 1,384.
For vocabulary see p. 107.

II. GOLDSMITH'S USE OF COLOR.

Text used: *Poems, Plays, and Essays.* 1 vol. Crowell.
Number of lines, 2,519.
For vocabulary see p. 107.

III.—COWPER'S USE OF COLOR.

Text used: *Poetical Works.* Benham edition. 1 vol. Macmillan, 1893.
Number of lines, 20,145.
For vocabulary see p. 107.

I.

Of Gray and Goldsmith as colorists there is little to say, since the total poetic output of each is so slight. Though the color-statistics of each may look interesting when reduced to percentages, the actual figures are meager; and we realize how misleading percentages may be when we see that Goldsmith's 26 per cent. of red, for example, is based upon only six uses of the hue, or that Gray's average of 64 color-words per 1,000 lines is computed from but 89 mentions of color in all of his verse.

Gray's verse, when we include the three poems which Gosse, in his edition of Gray's works, catalogues as "doubtful," and the translations from the Welsh and the Norse, amounts to but 1,921 lines; and when we omit the doubtful and translated poems, as I have here done, it becomes 1,384 lines, or about one-tenth of the verse which we may catalogue for Keats, the least prolific of the Romanticists. A comparison with the latter poet is naturally suggested by Gray's color-average of 64, falling but one word short of Keats's own; yet, apart from this relative wealth of usage, there is nothing whatever noteworthy in Gray's use of

33

color. Very little of his color is direct and real : the one poem in which we have more than isolated touches of concrete color is that on the *Favorite Cat*, where the hues are not exactly real, but are poetically heightened in much the same manner as are those of Chaucer's chanticleer (*Nonne Preestes Tale*, 39–44). If Gray uses his brush in a freer, more dainty, more decorative way than the typical Classicist of his century, his touch reminds us more of Spenser than it does of the Romanticists. He deals with abstractions and mythological imaginings oftener than with reality. Thus in Class A few of the hues go to man's actual body ; they are found, on the contrary, in such expressions as "rosy-bosomed Hours " (*Spring*, 1), "blue-eyed Pleasures " (*Poesy*, I, iii, 6), and "Envy wan " (*Eton*, 68). His Nature hues incline, in like manner, to the mythological. We have, it is true, one mention of "clear blue sky " (*Spring*, 9), and several lines where green is used of a real Nature (*Eton*, 23 ; *Poesy*, III, i, 2 ; *Vicissitude*, 8 ; *Sonnet* . . . . *West*, 4) ; but if we examine these in their context we shall find them in juxtaposition with "the purple year " (*Spring*, 4), "the hoary Thames along his silver-winding way" (*Eton*, 9–10), "The bloom of young Desire and Purple light of Love " (*Poesy*, I, iii, 17), the morning's "vermeil cheek" (*Vicissitude*, 3), and "red'ning Phœbus lifts his golden fire " (*Sonnet* . . . . *West*, 2). Gray's coloring, as a whole, is that of the Classicist, with some added daintiness. It does not anticipate the peculiar features of Romantic coloring in any respect save that of its high average of usage.

II.

Goldsmith is of all the poets here treated the most meager colorist. Twenty-three of his thirty-two poems are without a hint of color ; and in the remaining nine, color-terms occur but 26 times. Blue he uses not at all, yellow and purple but once, and Reds but six times, although they form his most numerous group. Only six of his color-lines refer to Nature. He uses color most frequently in Class B, dress — a fact which is amusingly paralleled by his instinct to deck himself in the tailor's brightest materials whenever a full purse allowed him such

indulgence. His color-touches seem altogether unstudied: one
could imagine them to be made almost unconsciously. They
are commonplace, stereotyped, realistic.

III.

Cowper's color is far more interesting and individual than
that of Gray or Goldsmith. To be sure, he uses it sparingly, but
his low average is due partly to the fact that his verse includes
such poems as the *Olney Hymns*, in whose 1,600 lines there is no
color at all.

The hues used by Cowper are almost always specific, applied
to steady and definite objects, and so described that they might
easily be represented by the painter. He seldom uses a color-
verb, or represents changing, fleeting hues. The correctness of
his observation of hues, as well as his remarkable memory for
them, must strike every reader of the *Task ;* yet he seldom quali-
fies colors — as Thomson, for instance, does — to afford us hints
of his taste. Perhaps "sober grey" (*Tirocinium*, 144) and "sight-
refreshing green" (*Task*, IV, 759) are the only expressions we
could count here. He does seem, however, to evince a fondness
for Reds, if we may judge by his frequent use of them. His
color-scale is the only one here noted that places Reds first and
subordinates Whites to the third rank (Tables V and VII).

In his distribution of color Cowper gives about one-
fourth to the human body, and devotes some attention to the
manufactured articles found in the interior of the home: in
treating these fields he is direct and true, but does not mass his
colors, or use them in variety, or go beyond the commonplace.
In Nature it is not the distant, or the grand, that wins his notice,
but the near, the small, the quiet object. He has left us no
color-record of mountain or forest, and next to none of waters.
His gently serious spirit found its joy in the things of which a
country home was the center — cultivated fields, woods but half
wild, and gardens of quiet retirement. His most notable color-
passages describe fruits, flowers, and trees. Upon these alone
does he lavish color deliberately and with delight. In sixty-three
lines of such description — *The Task*, I, 300–20 ; III, 570–80 ;

VI, 150–80 — can be found one-tenth of all the color Cowper uses. In these lines, too, appear his most careful discriminations of shade. The last passage is especially remarkable, since its richly-colored garden was not under the poet's eye, but was recreated from his memory while he listened to the "wintry music" of the wind among the barren shoots of January, and thought with hopeful faith how

> all this uniform uncoloured scene
> Shall be dismantled of its fleecy load
> And flush into variety again.

The passage in Book I is the only tree-list among the numerous ones found in poetry that dwells upon color, giving to the trees "each its hue peculiar." We see the gray smoothness of the ash and lime and beech, the "wannish grey" of the willow, the poplar's silver-lined leaf, the deepening shades of green which ash and elm and oak present, and

> The sycamore, capricious in attire,
> Now green, now tawny, and ere autumn yet
> Have changed the woods, in scarlet honours bright.

As I have said, the taste of Cowper did not lead him to describe the wild and grand, but the cultivated and the near. The trees noted above are not of the forest, but of the woodland next the sunburnt hayfield. So Cowper's flowers are all of the garden or the hedge-row. And the creatures of the animal world that claim any share of his color are either domesticated or directly associated with man : the peacock, "self-applauding bird" (*Truth*, 58) ; the pet bullfinch and his murderer, the "badger-coloured" rat (*Mrs. Throckmorton's Bullfinch*); the "downy gold" of the pheasant and the "river-blanched" snow of the swan, which helped to form *Mrs. Montagues' Feather-Hangings ;* the goldfinches that hung caged in the greenhouse ; and even the snake, whose "azure neck" the infant's playful hand shall stroke unharmed in the golden future of peace (*Task*, VI, 781). Cowper was ready to acknowledge that there is

> A soul in all things, and that soul is God.
> The beauties of the wilderness are His,

That make so gay the solitary place
Where no eye sees them,

but he could not refrain from showing the leanings of his own
gentle spirit in the lines that follow the above —

And the fairer forms,
That cultivation glories in, are His.

—Task, VI, 185–90.

CHAPTER V.

SCOTT'S USE OF COLOR.

Text used : *Poetical Works.* 1 vol. Fields, Osgood & Co., 1870.
Number of lines, 30,947.
For vocabulary see p. 108.

Scott is here treated before Coleridge and Wordsworth, not because his early poems antedate theirs, but because the taste for them on the part of the reading public was manifested decidedly earlier than the taste for the work of the Lake School. Just as Scott's novels and rimed romances appeal today to young people and to the youthful instincts of their elders, so they represent for us the youth of Romanticism — a youth in many respects obedient to its classical parents, but indulging in dreams and emotions that their authority could not curb.

As my tables show, Scott had a large color-vocabulary and used it lavishly. He also distributed his color impartially, giving about 50 per cent. each to Man and to Nature. In the wealth of his color he equals Shelley; in his color-vocabulary he falls little short of Shakspere. Therefore, when viewed simply from the numerical standpoint, his coloring possesses for us an unusual interest. Undoubtedly, too, he had a good eye and an honest affection for hue, whether he saw it in Man or in external Nature. He rejoiced in the Purples and Greens and Browns of Scotland's hills covered with heather and bracken, no less than in the snowy brow, crimson cheek, bonny black eye, and dark brown ringlets of Scotch maidens.

His vocabulary, which has its chief distinction in its Browns, is for the most part very simple, though it becomes large numerically by reason of his variants on the staple shades. Compare his Greens with Shelley's (pp. 108 and 110). Counting compounds, he has 12 Greens where Shelley has but 8. But Scott has in his list only three root-words, "emerald," "verdant," and

38

"green," with nine variants of green; while Shelley, with fewer variants, has all of the root-words of Scott, and in addition "chrysolite" and "glaucous." Scott's color, like his style in general, is clear, direct, and pictorial. He always prefers the term that will be perfectly clear to the average reader.

The significance of Scott's 48 words of color per 1,000 lines, here surpassed only by Keats's 65 (Table II), is somewhat lessened when we note how frequently his color is used for mere purposes of identification : in the true minstrel manner he often characterizes his person and landscape by the selection of some easily recognized, distinct quality—more often one of hue than of form—and holds to that as to a formula. Thus he introduces to us " Gray Morag," " Red Comyn," " Black Murthok," " Brown Maudlin," " Helias the White," etc., etc. And he carries his iterative formulæ into the realm of Nature, telling us at least 22 times that moonlight is "pale," 20 times that turrets and cloisters are "gray," and 15 times that the beacon-fire (not to speak of objects illuminated by it) is " red " or " ruddy."

The artistic value of Scott's abundant coloring also suffers from the fact that his color-words so frequently appear as rime words : "green" 78 times, "gray" 65, "red" 44, "blue" 37, "pale" 30, "white" 21, "brown" 19. These frequent occurrences in rime, constituting more than one-third of the total occurrences of the words named, leave it a matter of doubt whether Scott's main object in using them was not the securing of rimes. In Thomson's *Seasons*, where blank verse precludes the temptation to choose a word because its rime is needed, we have a much better index of the author's color-taste than in Scott's rimed tetrameters, for the shorter the rimed lines the more frequent the temptation. Yet, were we to make deductions from his percentages by allowing for his mechanically recurring color-formulæ, and for his color-rimes, Scott's verse would still remain rich in hues : it would still prove him true to his Scotch blood—a lineal descendant of such color-lovers as Gawain Douglas and James Thomson.

Scott liked brilliant or deep hues, broad contrasts, and strong lights and shadows. By means of these he constructed scenes in the main realistic, as they would appear to any observer

under everyday sunlight; though he had also a fondness for
securing unusual, and therefore telling, effects, by exhibiting
objects under artificial light, in colors not their own, and he
sometimes liked to assert the romancer's privilege of using the
"pencil wild" of Fantasy :

> For Fantasy embroiders Nature's veil.
> The tints of ruddy eve, or dawning pale,
> Of the swart thunder-cloud, or silver haze,
> Are but the ground-work of the rich detail
> Which Fantasy with pencil wild portrays,
> Blending what seems and is, in the rapt muser's gaze.
> —*Harold*, V, 1.

Scott has here given us one key to his own poetry. It is a
product of fancy, but of fancy blending what seems with what
is, building her castles, not in the vacant heaven as does Shelley,
but on the same substantial earth that his readers daily tread.
And in the construction of realistic scenes lit by the light of
fancy Scott has no more constant servant than color.

Ruskin (*loc. cit.*, III, pt. iv, chap. xvi, § 42) has called attention
to the fact that if Scott does not intend to say much about things,
the one character which he will give is color. Thus he paints
the sea-storm in the single line, "The blackening wave is edged
with white" (*Lay*, V.I, xxiii). Or he describes tents pitched
among the oak trees without mention of the form of either tent
or tree (*Marmion*, IV, xxv, 17). In the true manner of a modern
impressionist he gives the picture in broad strokes of the two
hues, white and green. One might multiply instances of clear,
positive, everyday hues laid on in the undefined washes and sharp
high-lights of the impressionistic scene-painter. (*The Lady of the
Lake*, I, xi, 1–6; I, xiv, 8–14; V, iii, 3; *Isles*, V, xiii, etc., etc.).
In the last passage referred to this is especially striking. The
passage also furnishes an instance of Scott's penchant for fire-
light scenes. A Schalken might revel in portraying the trial of
Constance de Beverley by the pale cresset's ray (*Marmion*, II, xix,
—), or the solitary figure of the abbot in *The Lord of the Isles*
(II, xxiii). Such bits in Scott frequently suggest the calcium
light and Bengal fire of the stage.

Scott, as before said, gives about one-half of his color to Nature. His work, standing as it does contemporary with that of Wordsworth and Shelley, naturally challenges comparison with theirs. Where, we ask, lies the difference between Scott's treatment of Nature and Wordsworth's? Or in what respect do his descriptions of lake and mountain and sky differ from Shelley's? To answer these questions fully, one would need to be naturalist, artist, and psychologist as well. But there are certain general differences between Scott's landscape and that of either of the poets just mentioned which reveal themselves to any reflecting reader. Wordsworth goes with reverence to Nature, loves her for her own sake, and in his poetry strives to reveal the power of her beauty and the beauty of her power. He is essentially a religious lyrist, and as such is concerned chiefly with the expression of his own mind, or with the interpretation of the mind of Nature, two things which with him are nearly synonymous. Shelley is in contact with the real universe only in so far as is necessary in order that he may construct for himself an impalpable, ideal universe, one in the picturing of which he may express his imaginative and emotional self. But Scott is neither a religious lyrist like Wordsworth, with his chief aim the faithful expression of himself and his relations to God's world; nor is he, like Shelley, the enraptured singer of an imaginary universe. He presents a real world, to real fellow-men as auditors and observers, and it is their minds rather than his own that constantly fill his thoughts and determine the character of his work.

Narratives like *Marmion* and *The Lady of the Lake* are essentially of the nature of the spectacular romantic drama, arranged to meet the comprehension and the approbation of the average mind. Here, as on the stage of the theater, we find formal exits and entrances, carefully chosen stage-setting and scenic detail, all the telling effects of moonlight, torchlight, and midnight beacon blaze; here also shifting companies of men and women —fair maidens, mailed warriors, gray palmers, courtly knights, hoary minstrels, and red villains; and connecting all a chain of sound, pleasant, musical verse, on the commonplace and healthful themes of fidelity and patriotism, of love and duty.

Scott's landscape is selected to give either suggestive and romantic, or historic setting to the action of his people. Take, for example, the opening canto of *Marmion*. The introduction will serve as a drop-curtain, the scene upon which we may study while we wait for the play to begin. On it is painted a November landscape — chill sky, a few sere red leaves on half-naked trees, a cascade foaming brown over rocks and through the glade, and sallow, russet-hued hills rising beyond. In the pale sunshine a flock of sheep crop the faded herbage, while their shepherd shiveringly wraps his mantle's fold closer, his dogs creeping close at his heels and casting cowering glances at the clouds. We

Feel the sad influence of the hour,

and fall to musing on dear departed joys. But we are not left to ourselves : the feelings appropriate to the scene the poet understands, and these he expresses for us through three hundred lines, until, expositor-wise, he announces

A knightly tale of Albion's elder day,

and the curtain rises. Before the action begins we have time to note the stage-setting for Act I (i, ii) — the Cheviot mountains, the river Tweed, and in the foreground Norham Castle whose embattled towers shine in the yellow luster of sunset. Warriors, pacing at guard upon the high turrets, are seen distinctly outlined against the evening sky, and their armor flashes back the western blaze in lines of dazzling light that fall athwart the gathering dusk. We are near enough to see that St. George's banner hangs heavily in the still air, and to hear faintly the old Border song hummed by the Warder, as he paces the gloomy portal arch above the barred gates.

And now the stage begins to fill — a herald on horseback, having blown his bugle-horn as he dashed up, announces the approach of Lord Marmion, and forty yeomen speed to unbar the iron-studded gates. Then appears Lord Marmion himself on his red-roan charger. We see the coal-black hair and mustache, here and there a bit grizzled, the eye of fire that flashes under his dark brow, and the warrior's scar on his brown cheek. He wears mail of shining Milan steel, and a falcon-crested helmet of burnished gold. On his shield appears again the falcon of his crest, sable in an azure field. And now we are bidden to observe that this azure hue is to be seen on all sides:

> Blue was the charger's broidered rein;
> Blue ribbons decked his arching mane;
> The knightly housing's ample fold
> Was velvet blue, and trapped with gold.

But the train of Lord Marmion is advancing. Behind the two gallant squires that immediately follow him come four men-at-arms, the last one bearing his master's "forky pennon."

> Like swallow's tail, in shape and hue,
> Fluttered the streamer, glossy blue,
> Where, blazoned sable, as before,
> The towering falcon seemed to soar.
> Last, twenty yeomen, two and two,
> In hosen black, and jerkins blue,
> With falcons broidered on each breast,
> Attended on their lord's behest.

After a flourish of trumpets, two pursuivants hail Lord Marmion, and marshal him to the castle hall, into which he and his train disappear as the herald loudly cries,

> " Room, lordlings, room for Lord Marmion,
> With the crest and helm of gold!"

Here everything is admirably arranged for spectacular effect. Each detail could be represented upon the stage. The people are brought on in approved theatrical manner; the few colors are clear and strong, contrasted yet harmonious.

If we failed at first to understand the purport of the scene on the drop-curtain, we are no longer in doubt when once we have followed Lord Marmion into the castle and witnessed the coolness that underlies the courteous manner of both host and guest. The gray desolation of the prefatory scene struck the keynote of the succeeding action.

We must not linger on this dramatic phase of Scott's work, though we may note in passing how fully the next canto of *Mar-*

mion bears out our deductions from the first canto. There the drop-curtain has two contrasted scenes—one showing a lonely thorn standing sentinel over waste glens; the other, the same spot clothed, as it once was, with a fair forest through which leap the red deer, followed by gallant greyhounds and merry hunters. The poet again expresses for us the sentiments of the scene. Then follow a succession of tableaux in which we see a bark containing the Abbess of St. Hilda and nine nuns cross the North seas from Whitby. As they reach the Holy Isle, the nuns sing St. Hilda's song, and down from the "solemn, huge, and dark-red" monastery of St. Cuthbert file the monks and nuns to welcome their sisters, while

> Conspicuous by her veil and hood,
> Signing her cross, the Abbess stood
> And blessed them with her hand.

As we follow the canto through we guess why the poet gave us on the drop-curtain those two contrasted scenes—the one full of green and lusty life, the other waste and gray. It was to prepare us for the scenes within the monastery walls; for there, while the Whitby nuns and St. Cuthbert's daughters close round the fire in the high rooms that overlook the sea and with pious exultation

> · all, in turn, essay to paint
> The rival merits of their saint,

the fearful tragedy of Constance de Beverley's trial and murder is being enacted in a secret aisle beneath. These two scenes, so wide apart in their messages to human hearts, the one so full of innocent pleasure and holy peace, the other so intensely and pathetically tragic, are put before us simultaneously. It is as if the poet had in mind such a two-storied stage as that of the old miracle pageants, where men and demons were acting below, while saints and angels went through their parts above.

I have dwelt upon these cantos somewhat at length because they exhibit so clearly the dramatic and spectacular instinct that underlies all of Scott's work. His men and women are of chief importance to him, Nature being made, in almost every case, to serve as a background for human emotions or human deeds. Scenes are chosen which will give an appropriate setting—historic, or romantic, or symbolic—to the *dramatis personæ*. As the story develops, the scenes, of course, shift, the poet always giving us a moment's pause that we may catch the main features of the new background. Such a beautiful scene, for example, as that disclosed at the beginning of *The Lady of the Lake* has its dramatic justification, not so much in its intrinsic beauty as in the fitting romantic background which it supplies for the figures of hero and heroine about to appear. It goes farther than the mere furnishing of stage scenery: it strikes the keynote of peace and love that is to dominate the intercourse of Fitz James and Ellen.

And Scott's use of color shows, in little, the same traits and the same underlying purpose that are manifest in his dramatic narrative as a whole. Wordsworth's coloring is emotional and yet pervaded with the soul-truthfulness of a steady mind and a steady eye. Shelley's coloring is emotional, nascent, in a constant state of change—imaginatively true but subtle rather than realistic. Scott's colors are fresh, distinct, steady, true to the actual hues of the world about us; and they are handled by Scott as the costumer and scene-painter would handle his colors in setting a play. They exhibit the same appeal to the romantic feelings of the reader, through devices naïvely artificial and addressed to the senses rather than to the mind; the same compound of freshness and of conventionality, of limelight and of sunlight; and the same striving after scenic effect in the unfolding of the narrative.

CHAPTER VI.

COLERIDGE'S USE OF COLOR.

Text used : *Poetical Works.* 1 vol. Macmillan, 1873.
Number of lines, 20,189.
For vocabulary see p. 108.

If we consult the comparative tables to learn how Coleridge stands as a colorist, we shall see that both in extent of vocabulary (Table I) and in amount of color-usage (Table II) he strikes almost the exact average of thepoets there represented. Further, when we limit our comparison to poets of his own school, it will appear that, despite his rather meager coloring, Coleridge comes very near to the average color-scale (Table V) of the Romanticists. The proportions in which he distributes his colors between Man, Nature, and abstractions vary only 1–2 per cent. from the Romantic average,[1] as will be seen from the subjoined condensation of Table VII :

	Man	Nature	Abstractions, etc.
Scott,	50	48	2
Coleridge,	39	55	6
Wordsworth,	26	72	2
Byron,	58	33	9
Shelley,	31	63	6
Keats,	41	54	5
Average	41	54	5

This intermediate position of Coleridge as regards the larger range of English verse is not only apparent, but real ; he clasps hands with both predecessors and contemporaries, uniting in

[1] For other periods we have these figures :

	Man	Nature	Abstractions, etc.
Langland, Gower, and Chaucer,	54	36	10
Spenser and Shakspere,	63	29	8
Pope,	23	47	10

himself, as we shall see later, the color-methods of Classicist and Romanticist.[1]

Keats, as the first of the condensed tables on p. 46 shows, approximates even more nearly than Coleridge to the mean color-distribution of the Romantic Period ; and therefore, if we are to lay any stress upon the agreement of Coleridge's average with that of his school, we shall have to explain the same fact for Keats. In the case of Keats, however, we have, throughout his few years of poetic production, a uniform and impartial interest in both Man and Nature. The coincidence of his color-average with that of his school may be exemplified in detached portions of his work as well as in the whole ; it represents a full, sustained, and spontaneous affection for all the aspects of the world he studied.

Coleridge's agreement with the average, on the other hand, is not to be explained as a steady impartiality of affection. The student of his work as a whole finds that his interest in color is not sustained, but that he shows now one preference, now another. Broadly speaking, his verse falls into two classes — that produced before and that produced after 1796. In the former he is conventional and unspontaneous, imitative, by Romantic instinct, of the earlier non-classical poets, Spenser, Milton, Gray, and Bowles, but proving his immaturity by the "classic" slavishness of that imitation. In the latter period, after his marriage, and after his friendship with Wordsworth was formed, Coleridge produced all of his best and most characteristic work. Thus his agreement with the Romantic average is not, as in the case of, Keats, the result of a steady, balanced richness of production but of the equalizing of two different tendencies, the one imitative of an earlier period in which Man was the important object, the other in harmony with the predominant Nature interest of his own time.

[1] Since writing the above I have with interest noted what Mr. Richard Garnett says in the introduction to his recent edition of *The Poetical Works of Coleridge* — that Coleridge is "the incarnate transition, so to speak, from the eighteenth to the nineteenth century. . . . The poetries of the eighteenth and nineteenth centuries lie associated within the covers of his writings. . . . He has the unique distinction among the singers of his time of himself exemplifying the antagonistic styles within the limits of his own verse."

I have called Coleridge's early color imitative, for this great
borrower was but too likely, wherever he found in the pages of
another an idea with which he fully agreed, to appropriate both
the spirit and the form of the idea. Of the borrowings in his
verse less has been said than of those in his prose. Yet the
early poems are full of verbal echoes of the poets who happened
from time to time to occupy his thoughts. Sometimes the echo
is heard in the swing of the verse — *e. g.*, in the *Destruction
of the Bastile* the influence of Gray's odes is unmistakable ;
sometimes it comes in the prevailing sentiment — *e. g.*, the sonnets *The Tear which Mourned* and *I too a Sister had* recall
the pensive manner of Bowles; sometimes borrowed word and
phrase are blended with his own in such a way that they can
hardly be disentangled, yet so that they recall to the reader
Spenser, or Milton, Gray, Bowles, or Wordsworth — *e. g.*, stanza
vi, in *Dejection*, which manifestly echoes Wordsworth's *Ode
. . . . Immortality;* or the *Song of the Pixies* and *Lines on an
Autumnal Evening*, whose subtle echoes of *Comus* and *Il Penseroso*
Brandl has noted (*loc. cit.*, 83). In his manner of using other
authors, Coleridge stands midway between a man like William
Godwin, whose pages are sprinkled with direct quotations from
the Bible, Shakspere, and other well-known sources, and a man
like Charles Lamb, half the charm of whose essays lies in their
"quotations in solution." Coleridge's borrowings are neither
frankly acknowledged, nor so fully recast by his genius as to
make acknowledgment unnecessary. They are in a state of
semi-solution.

We are here concerned, however, with those borrowings only
which contain words of color. They are found chiefly in the
poems written before 1796. Here Coleridge shows himself a verit-
able chameleon, unconsciously taking the color of that upon which
he feeds. His "amber" (*Autumnal Evening*, 4 ; *Lewti*, 21) seems
to be an echo of Milton's *L'Allegro*, 61 ; "sable" (*Pixies*, 84), of
Paradise Lost, II, 962; "sable" (*Teakettle*, 35), the "black" of *Il Penseroso*, 17; "pale ivy" (*Pixies*, 30) of Spenser's *Virgil's Gnat*, 222,
675, as that was of Virgil's "*pallente hedera.*" His description of
the glow-worm in *Shurton Bars*, 5, Coleridge himself, in a note,

acknowledges to be taken from Wordsworth's *An Evening Walk*
(version of 1793); while it is commonly known that the "brown"
hand of the Ancient Mariner was a touch added by Wordsworth.
There are also debts to Dorothy Wordsworth's *Journal* for January and March, 1798, in the stanzas added to *Christabel* a year after
it was first written (*e. g.*, the "thin grey cloud," l. 16 ; the "one red
leaf," l. 49), though, as they record observations made by the
Wordsworths and Coleridge together, it is only just to consider
them touches to which the latter had a perfect right. And an
obvious borrowing from Bowles's

> How sweet the tuneful bell's responsive peal!
> As when, at opening morn, the fragrant breeze
> Breathes on the trembling sense of pale disease,
>
> (*The Bells, Ostend*),

is found in Coleridge's lines

> But ah! not music's self, nor fragrant bower,
> Can glad the trembling sense of wan disease.
>
> —*Pain*, 3-4.

In Coleridge's early verse colors are either borrowed, as in the
cases above cited, or embalmed in trite phrases and mythological
commonplaces that would be wholly in keeping with Pope's imi-
tators: "coal-black steed," "red ruin," "purple Pride," "white-
robed Purity," "pallid Fear," "black tide of death," etc., etc.
Had Coleridge's color-sense been full and a source of especial
pleasure to him, it is not likely that he would have so easily
accepted lines at second-hand. But it is almost certain that his
greater sense-pleasures lay elsewhere. Sounds, for instance,
appealed to him more than hues did. We have one natural bit
of color-recollection in the *Sonnet to the Otter*, but with that
exception it is not until the stimulus of Sara's love and Wordsworth's friendship combine to arouse his independent self to
action that Coleridge ceases to look through the eyes of others and
tells us frankly what he sees with his own. He then writes poems
like *The Eolian Harp* and *Reflections on . . . . Retirement*, in which
we find very little color, it is true, but in which that little bears
the stamp of reality.

From this time on, in the poems which are generally adjudged the truest expressions of Coleridge's genius, the neutral-tinted abstractions and echoed commonplaces of color decrease. We find in their places either realistic colors recorded by an observant eye, or intense and unnatural hues deliberately employed to produce an effect of the supernatural. The latter may be seen in *The Ancient Mariner*, whose weird effects are heightened by the "copper sky," the "bloody sun," the water that "burned green, and blue, and white," the sailors' "black lips baked," the skin of Life-in-Death, "white as leprosy," the "still and awful red" of the ship's huge shadow, the water snakes in their "rich attire, blue, glossy-green, and velvet black," and the uncanny mystery of the "crimson" specters which came rising from the bay that was "white with silent light."

Here Coleridge is no imitator; he is original, creative. And he is quite as far from imitation in the few passages where he has taken pains to record his observations of Nature's true colors. The most notable of these are the two following:

> A curious picture, with a master's haste
> Sketched on a strip of pinky-silver skin
> Peeled from the birchen bark-!
>
> —*The Picture*, 159-61.

> All this long eve, so balmy and serene,
>   Have I been gazing on the western sky,
>   And its peculiar tint of yellow-green:
>   And still I gaze — and with how blank an eye!
> And those thin clouds above, in flakes and bars,
> That give away their motion to the stars;
> Those stars, that glide behind them or between,
> Now sparkling, now bedimmed, but always seen;
> Yon crescent moon, as fixed as if it grew
> In its own cloudless, starless lake of blue;
> I see, not feel, how beautiful they are!
>   My genial spirits fail;
>   And what can these avail
> To lift the smothering weight from off my breast?
>   It were a vain endeavour,
>   Though I should gaze forever
> On that green light that lingers in the west:

I may not hope from outward forms to win
The passion and the life, whose fountains are within.
—*Dejection*, 27-46.

The last citation is a suitable one with which to close an account of Coleridge's color, since it contains his most careful color-study—of the evening sky's "peculiar tint of yellow-green," —and at the same time contains his acknowledgment that, gaze though he may forever on that green light, it is from other founts that he must draw the inspiration which color fails to afford him. Like Wordsworth, Coleridge is unable to find in color the full satisfaction of an æsthetic sense which in Wordsworth was strongly moral, and in himself was more susceptible to the law underlying beauty than to the beauty itself. The hymning of color as color, the attribution of vital divinity to the pure hue, has been reserved for our own time and for Mr. George Meredith.

CHAPTER VII.

WORDSWORTH'S USE OF COLOR.

Text used : *Poetical Works.* 1 vol. Macmillan, 1891.
Number of lines, 53,343.
For vocabulary see p. 109.

Knowing Wordsworth's love for Nature and his fidelity to her teachings, we come to the study of his poetry with a reasonable expectation of finding his colors, so far as he may employ them, true to the time, the place, and the object described. Knowing, too, his unswerving conscientiousness in the recording of his own thoughts and feelings, we are also justified in the expectation that, if he has any definite opinions on the subject of color in general, or any strong feeling for individual colors, such opinion or feeling will find mention in his self-analytic verse. In another poet, absence of comment as to the influence of some special phase of Nature upon his own emotions might count for nothing ; in a man like Wordsworth, who so studiously searched his mind for the truths that nature had impressed there, failure to mention such an influence argues a failure to feel it — certainly a failure to feel it in any strength.

Our first expectation is abundantly fulfilled. From *An Evening Walk*, written before the poet was twenty, to the lines *Suggested by a Picture of the Bird of Paradise*, written when he was seventy-five, the strokes of color are plainly the result of personal observation, and are both truthful and suggestive, both real and idealized. Unlike Coleridge and Byron, Wordsworth passed through no period of immaturity in his observations of external Nature. His understanding of her depths of significance was reached only after a long period of study, but from the first his eye was accurate and his mind unbiased by book-knowledge; and this individuality and honesty are evident in his use of color. On the second point, Wordsworth's direct recognition of

color as an influence, potent or impotent, in the development of
his inner self, we naturally seek for evidence in his autobio-
graphic poems, particularly in Books I, II, IV, and XII of the
Prelude.

Looking back with reverential joy to the "fair seed-time" of
his soul, Wordsworth tells us in Book I some of the "remember-
able things" that the earth and common face of Nature spoke to
him. We may pass over the personal activities, those "glad animal movements" (*Tintern,* 74) that naturally form a large part
of the memories of a healthy boyhood.[1] In addition to these
memories of activities bound up with his own being, Wordsworth
describes many impressions received from without. Those
recalled with especial keenness and joy may be classified under
the three heads: (1) Sound (with silence), (2) Motion (with
rest), (3) Light (with shadow). Sometimes these memories
stand out separately, sometimes they are blended; but always
they are described with the delicate accuracy of the poet who
possesses

> a watchful heart
> Still couchant, an inevitable ear,
> And an eye practiced like a blind man's touch.
> — *When to the attractions* . . . . , 81–3.

These memories were directly associated for Wordsworth with
his higher, holier intercourse with Nature and with that Spirit of
the Universe which gives "to forms and images a breath and
everlasting motion" (*Prel.,* I, 403). They spoke to him of a conscious prompting soul behind "silent Nature's breathing life"
(*Peele,* 28), and imparted to his own life mystery and grandeur,
"inward hopes and swellings of the spirit" (*Prel.,* IV, 163).

The first book of the *Prelude* furnishes many instances of
Wordsworth's "inevitable ear," and of the effect upon him both
of movements, real and apparent, in the external world, and of
"light and shade, each ministering to each."[2]

To a heart so early stirred with the belief that all visible

[1] These may be indicated by the verbs employed in *Prel.,* I, 291–316:
bask, plunge, scour, leap, run, sport, range, scud, ply.

[2] See ll. 269–78, 336–9, 375–90, 433–44, 539–43, 559–72, 568–80.

things "respired with inner meaning" (*Prel.*, III, 132) is it
strange that forms and colors, especially where these were not
subject to growth or change, were less significant than

> the clouds,
> The mist, the shadows, light of golden suns,
> Motions of moonlight   (*Excursion*, II, 712-14),

and "the soul of happy sound" (*Peter*, I, 67)? One citation
must serve to illustrate Wordsworth's feeling for the sounds and
motions of Nature, though an overwhelming number might be
found in its support :

> Ye motions of delight, that haunt the sides
> Of the green hills ; ye breezes and soft airs
> Whose subtle intercourse with breathing flowers,
> Feelingly watched, might teach Man's haughty race
> How without injury to take, to give
> Without offence ; ye who, as if to show
> The wondrous influence of power gently used,
> Bend the complying heads of lordly pines,
> And, with a touch, shift the stupendous clouds
> Through the whole compass of the sky ; ye brooks,
> Muttering along the stones, a busy noise
> By day, a quiet sound in silent night ;
> Ye waves, that out of the great deep steal forth
> In a calm hour to kiss the pebbly shore,
> Not mute, and then retire, fearing no storm ;
> And you, ye groves, whose ministry it is
> To interpose the covert of your shades,
> Even as a sleep, between the heart of man
> And outward troubles, between man himself,
> Not seldom, and his own uneasy heart :
> Oh ! that I had a music and a voice
> Harmonious as your own, that I might tell
> What ye have done for me.
> —*Prel.*, XII, 9 ff.

But where shall we find in Wordsworth's poetry joy in color
at all commensurate with this joy in sound and motion ? Once,
indeed, when gazing at the full-flowered broom upon the steep,
he delights

> To note in shrub and tree, in stone and flower,
> That intermixture of delicious hues
> Along so vast a surface, all at once,
> In one impression, by connecting force
> Of their own beauty, imaged on the heart
>
>   (*To Joanna*, 46 ff.);

but such passages are very infrequent, while we might fill many pages with exquisite expressions of his passion for that

> . . . . something far more deeply interfused,
> Whose dwelling is the light of setting suns,
> And the round ocean and the living air,
> And the blue sky, and in the mind of man.
>
>   -— *Tintern*, 96.

He tells us that the scenes which were the witness of his boyish activities became " habitually dear " and that " all their forms and changeful colours " were fastened to his affections (*Prel.*, I, 609–12). This affection for forms and colors was, however, distinctly subordinate to his love for murmuring wind and stream, or for the " soft eye-music of slow-waving boughs " (*Airey-Force*, 14), or for the

>   lights and shades
> That marched and countermarched about the hills
> In glorious apparition
>
>   (*Prel.*, XII, 96–8),

a fact which is especially true of sounds, and notably of the murmuring of streams, his enjoyment of which is omnipresent in his verse : it formed his earliest recollection (*Prel.*, I, 270), and in his seventy-seventh year he was still convinced that

> That voice of unpretending harmony
> *   *   *   *   *   *   *   *
> Wants not a healing influence that can creep
> Into the human breast.
>
>   -— *The unremitting voice*, 6 ff.

But, in contrast with the voice of wind and stream, forms and colors were to him external qualities, Nature's dress rather than utterances of her life : and for this reason, though they appealed to Wordsworth's eye and were mingled with happy memories, they meant less and less to him as his mind became more mature and more watchful for "the latent qualities and essences of things" (*Prel.*, II, 325).

This we may prove for his colors in two ways, numerically and by citations.

Take first the citations. In *Lines composed . . . . above Tintern Abbey*, written in 1798, is found this reference to the author's "boyish days" (the *italics* are mine):

> I cannot paint
> What then I was.   The sounding cataract
> Haunted me like a passion; the tall rock,
> The mountain, and the deep and gloomy wood,
> *Their colours and their forms, were then to me*
> *An appetite; a feeling and a love,*
> *That had no need of a remoter charm,*
> *By thought supplied, nor any interest*
> *Unborrowed from the eye.—That time is past.*

In the *Prelude*, after we have learned of Wordsworth's early affection for "forms and changeful colours" (I, 611), and of the gradual weakening of those "incidental charms" which first attached his heart to rural objects (II, 198), we come, at length, to these self-reproachful lines:

> O Soul of Nature! that, by laws divine
> Sustained and governed, still dost overflow
> With an impassioned life, what feeble ones
> Walk on this earth! how feeble have I been
> When thou wert in thy strength!
> * .   *   *   *   *   *
> *Bent overmuch on superficial things,*
> *Pampering myself with meagre novelties*
> *Of colour and proportion ;*[1] to the moods
> Of time and season, to the moral power,
> The affections and the spirit of the place
> Insensible. . . . .
> *   *   *   *   *   *
> I speak in recollection of a time
> When the bodily eye, in every stage of life

[1] The *italics* are again mine, except in the case of the word *me*, line 130.

> The most despotic of our senses, gained
> Such strength in *me* as often held my mind
> In absolute dominion.
>
> —*Prel.*, XII, 102 ff.
>
> As the horizon of my mind enlarged
> Again I took the intellectual eye
> For my instructor, studious more to see
> Great truths, than touch and handle little ones.
>
> —*Prel.*, XIII, 51 ff.

We have, therefore, the poet's own account of his emancipation from the tyranny of the bodily eye and from a taste for the meager novelties of color and proportion.

As for a Peter Bell—

> The primrose by the river's brim
> A *yellow* primrose was to him,
> And it was nothing more.

Peter got from the flower simply and solely a color-impression, never "thoughts that do lie too deep for tears." He was therefore counted dull indeed of sense by a poet like Wordsworth, the appetite of whose childish mind for external beauties was so early and so fully transcended by the bliss ineffable of communion with the God of Nature.

The gradual diminution in Wordsworth's color-interest may also be proven numerically by a comparison of the amounts of color used at different periods of his life. For example, the color-average of the poems written before 1796 is 38 words per 1,000 lines; that of the poems after 1830, 13 words per 1,000 lines. Again, we may take the records of his three continental tours—those of 1793, 1820, and 1837,—which are suited to our purpose because of nearly the same lengths, on similar subjects, and representative of three stages of his work and thought. The first group has in each 1,000 lines 65 color-words, the second 32, the third 13.

We must therefore be careful not to estimate Wordsworth as a colorist by such early poems as *An Evening Walk* and *Descriptive Sketches*, which employ color as lavishly as do the early poems of Keats. The mind that

difference
Perceived in things, where, to the unwatchful eye,
No difference is

(*Prel.*, II, 299-301),

Wordsworth never lost. But he chose to exercise it less and less
in the domain of color, and more and more in the subtler
domains of Nature.

I have dwelt on Wordsworth's subordination of color-percep-
tions to other sense-perceptions more directly exhibiting the
immanence of divine life in Nature, because this fact, when fully
understood, becomes a key to his chief traits as a colorist. He
was a worshiper of Nature's soul, loving every slightest token
of its life. Such tokens he found not alone in Nature's motions
and sounds, but also in her silence and repose ; for these did not
speak to him of absence of life, but of life perfectly poised and
controlled. In his times of inward turmoil, Nature restored him
to "happy stillness" by her soothing calm ; in times when his
will and purpose lapsed, contact with her vigorous life gave him
energy to renew his search for truth. These two moods he himself recognized :

From Nature doth emotions come, and moods
Of calmness equally are Nature's gift :
This is her glory ; these two attributes
Are sister horns that constitute her strength.
—*Prel.*, XIII, 1-4.

These two attributes, translated into color, represent Wordsworth's strongest preferences in this field : the immortal Greens,
forever quiet yet forever bearing witness of the earth's rejuvena-
tion; shining Whites or Golds associated with the streaming lights
of the sun, " pledge and surcty of our earthly iife (a light which
we behold and feel we are alive)"; and the placid Blues of
dimpling lake or cloudless sky.

To even these hues, however, he seldom gives more than
a brief mention. They are never apostrophized as are the
sounds of streams, the rhythmic movements of a wind-stirred
tree, or the gleam of sun-lit water and curling mists. They

constitute a pleasing but subordinate part of the scenes with which his memory is stored.

"Green" is his most frequent color-word, and it is the green of the plant world: 275 of his 295 uses of the hue are applied directly to vegetation. It holds a larger place in his later work than in his earlier, constituting only 18 per cent. of his color in poems written before 1798, but 30 per cent. of those after 1830.

"Blue" ranks second among his terms for bright color, and with this, as with "green," we have a strongly predominant association with certain things. In 69 of its 89 occurrences it describes lake or sky.

Yellows were pleasing to him when they had luster, as seen in lines like these:

> The sun, above the mountain's head,
> A freshening lustre mellow
> Through all the long green fields had spread,
> His first sweet evening yellow.
>   —*Tables Turned*, 4–8.[1]

Purple occurs with frequency in his early poems, but with a touch of conventionality. Later it is neglected, but its few occurrences bear the stamp of reality.

It is in the number of his compounds of green and of blue that Wordsworth's color-vocabulary is most individual, *e. g.*, "olive-green" and "pea-green" moss, "tawny-green" vegetation, a "black-blue" sky, the "sapphire-blue" eye-bright.

His hues are usually perfectly natural.[2] In the few cases where they are heightened or over-emphasized it is with an aim at supernatural effect, an aim restricted to a very small portion of Wordsworth's work, and to poems written apparently under the influence of Coleridge's example. These poems are *Peter Bell* and *The Thorn*, both included in the *Lyrical Ballads*, and *The White Doe*, written in 1807. In *Peter Bell* we have impossible effects in blue and gray and tender green in the deserted

[1] See also *Excursion*, I, 718; IV, 1302; VII, 876; *Desc. Sketches*, 95; *Prel.*, VIII, 463; *Joanna*, 40.

[2] We may perhaps except his "dark-brown shadows," and some rather conventional Purples.

quarry on a moonlit night; in *The Thorn* we have mosses of
extraordinary brilliancy covering an infant's grave; and in *The
White Doe* the intense whiteness and radiance of the creature
is so persistently dwelt upon that the repetition at last creates
an uncanny impression in the reader's mind.

Such use of color is, however, rare in Wordsworth. His
color as a whole is truthful and discriminating. It is to a
marked degree expended upon external Nature to the neglect of
Man. It is cold rather than warm, and is most enjoyed when
accompanied by luster and radiance. Abundant in his earliest
poems, it drops in his latest to a percentage as low as Cowper's.
As a whole he is less lavish of it than is any other of the
Romantic poets; and in his own esteem it is plainly an incidental
and superficial quality, speaking God's message to the heart of
man less directly than do mountain shadows, moving clouds, the
smile of sunshine on mists and waters, or the music of wind
and stream.

CHAPTER VIII.

BYRON'S USE OF COLOR.

Text used : *Poems and Dramas.* 1 vol. Crowell & Co., New York.
Number of lines, 59,999.
For vocabulary see pp. 109-10.

Among the English Romantic poets Byron stands first in the amount of his poetic production. In the thirty-two years of his life he published more verse than either Scott or Coleridge, Shelley or Keats, and nearly seven thousand lines more than did Wordsworth in his long life of fourscore years.

With so large a body of work from which to draw conclusions, we may speak with some assurance as to Byron's feeling for color and his manner of using it. Brief as was his period of production — only about eighteen years — his genius matured so rapidly, and took on so early its characteristic traits, that the work of his short life may reasonably be studied as a growth, in accordance with the features of its development.

Two events in his life are of great moment because of the bent which each gave to his mind and his passions ; and the dates at which these events occurred therefore form convenient lines of demarcation in his color-treatment. The first of these is his " grand tour " to the continent in 1809-11, a tour which removed his thoughts from the subjects treated in *English Bards and Scotch Reviewers*, and turned them to the interests in travel and in foreign scenes which inspired almost all his best and most characteristic work. The second event is his flight from England in 1816, after the scandal occasioned by his separation from the woman who had been but one year his wife. This separation, causing as it did an unparalleled amount of discussion and censure in English society, and arousing against Byron the prejudices and suspicions of the English public, embittered the remaining years of the poet's life, and gave to his already egoistic verse a satiric recklessness, a scorn of social conventions, and even of humanity, which set *Beppo* and *Don Juan* effectually apart from *Childe Harold*, the *Prisoner of Chillon*, and the *Siege of Corinth*.

Previous to his first journey abroad he published *Hours of Idleness* and *English Bards and Scotch Reviewers*—a body of work distinctly conventional and commonplace in sentiment, though clever and facile in execution. The color-treatment of this early work is of the same stamp, unoriginal and mannered both in vocabulary and in application. Of the few poems in this first volume which mention hues, *Oscar of Alva* is the chief, and here the influence of Scott's ballads is evident in lines like:

> Where Alva's hoary turrets rise.
>
> Or roll the crimson tide of war.
>
> Dark was the flow of Oscar's hair.
>
> Glenalvon's blue-eyed daughter came.
>
> The crimson glow of Allan's face
> Was turned at once to ghastly hue.
>
> A form was seen in tartan green.
>
> Dark Oscar's sable crest is low.
>
> What minstrel gray, what hoary bard
> Shall Allan's deeds on harpstrings raise.

In the prose imitation of Ossian, included in the same volume, there is also a decidedly imitative use of color and color-formulæ; and the hues employed in *English Bards* reflect exactly the mannerisms of Pope, Byron's model in the composition of the satire. Such original color-treatment as remains after the exclusion of stereotyped expressions like " Health's rosy wing," "the sable hues of Grief," "the rosy finger of the morn," is scanty indeed, but is nevertheless sufficient to show Byron's dawning interest in the hues of eyes, hair, and skin, and his love of the " dark-blue deep." We should, perhaps, not emphasize the predominance of these two color-interests over other color-usages, were it not that we have here, foreshadowed, even though dimly, the characteristic color-interest of Byron's verse as a whole.

In noting, therefore, the distinctive features of this early and immature period in Byron's work, we find, first, a general meagerness and conventionality of coloring ; and, second, a predominant interest in Man rather than in Nature. For the earth was not, to Byron's boyish mind, as to Thomson's, one vast

> innumerous-colour'd scene of things.

When Byron writes of his *Childish Recollections*, he is ruled almost entirely by classic conventions of thought and phraseology, and the one color-touch of the 412 lines of this poem which we can feel was a part of real experience is contained in the line

> plunging from the green declining shore,

in which he describes his pleasure in swimming. And, thirdly, in our list of the color-characteristics indicated in these early poems, we have his enjoyment of the hues of large expanses of water. The "dark-blue" of the sea, so omnipresent in his maturer work, appears already in *Dorset*, 89 ; *I would I were*, 4 ; *To Florence*, 10 ; *Thunderstorm*, 56.

Aside, then, from the barrenness of the first productive period, which we select as one of its three characteristics, we see hinted two color-preferences on the poet's part, an interest in Man rather than Nature, and a strong feeling for the color of the sea or of large expanses of water. These two lines of interest developed so markedly in Byron's maturer poetry, and form so large a part of his color-applications, that were we to remove from his verse the color-terms which he applies to man's face and form, and those he applies to the sea, he would lose 48 of the 111 words of his vocabulary, and 50 per cent. of his entire color. Of these 48 terms, 5 only belong to the sea ; the remaining 43, running all through the scale from "pomegranate" to "purple-hectic," and from "swanlike" to "inky," are used in describing the face and hair of man (or woman) (see Chart A).

As before remarked, Byron's first continental tour had a decided influence upon his mind and genius. He had hitherto been imitative and trite in both thought and phraseology, but in contact with foreign scenes and peoples he found a stimulus under which his mind awoke to originality and power. From

this time, 1809–11, while his interest in Man remains predominant, and he never tires of the "dark-blue ocean," Byron
shows a widening interest in Nature's hues, and a more genuine
and natural manner of using them. This is best seen in *Childe
Harold*, whose early cantos were published by Murray in 1812,
and first revealed to the English public the fact that a new
poetic star had risen. Though this poem was continued some
years later, and after work of quite a different tone was dividing
with it the author's interest, its spirit is so consistent throughout
that we may be justified in considering it as a whole, and a whole
produced under the impulses gained before Byron's reputation
suffered so fierce a reverse in 1816.

The first colors in *Childe Harold* strike the keynote of Byron's
early interests, when he speaks of

> The laughing dames in whom he did delight,
> Whose large blue eyes, fair locks, and snowy hands,
> Might shake the saintship of an anchorite
>
> (I, xi);

and then cries,

> Welcome, welcome, ye dark-blue waves!
>
> —I, :xiii, 10.

That is, he begins on the old key of human and of ocean description. But soon we feel a new atmosphere about us. The trav-
eler finds as he approaches the shores of Spain that

> it is a goodly sight to see
> What Heaven hath done for this delicious land !
> What fruits of fragrance blush on every tree!
> What goodly prospects o'er the hills expand !
>
> —I, xv.

Byron now begins to notice the beauty of a particular Nature-
scene and to describe it with his eye on the object, as in I, xix;
II, xvii, xlii, xlviii–xlix, li–lii. In such descriptions his power
does not lie so much in the form or color of specific objects as in
the skill with which he groups them. He thus secures fine effects
in the general composition of his pictures, but his detail is likely
to be vague and evasive. An artist illustrating the *Childe Harold*
would find the general hues of large expanses given him fre-

quently by the poet: skies "azure" or "blue;" waters "azure,"
"blue," "dark-blue," "green" or "deep green," "dun," "gray" or
simply "dark;" forests "green," "hoar," "dark," "black"—but
in details he would be unrestricted. Byron's color-interest, so
far as it is given to Nature, is notably weak in the direction of
minutiæ. To the hues of animals and flowers no poet whom I
have studied pays so little heed (see D–F, Table VII). His whole
bouquet contains but one "deep-blue" violet and two roses,
"purple" and "white." And his list of animal hues is almost
as brief. For the small objects of the outside world he seems
to have had little affection, here forming the strongest contrast
to a man like Cowper, whose most attractive bits of Nature study
are devoted to birds and flowers.

But if neglectful of Nature's smaller details and more delicate
manifestations, Byron expressed strong love for her in her more
general aspects and wilder moods:

> Oh! she is fairest in her features wild,
> Where nothing polished dares pollute her path:
> To me by day or night she ever smiled,
> Though I have marked her where none other hath
> And sought her more and more, and loved her best in wrath.
> —Childe Harold, II, xxxvii.

> Where rose the mountains, there to him were friends,
> Where rolled the ocean, thereon was his home.
> —III, xiii.

> Are not the mountains, waves, and skies, a part
> Of me and of my soul, as I of them?
> Is not the love of these deep in my heart
> With a pure passion? Should I not contemn
> All objects, if compared with these?
> —III, lxxv.

> Oh night,
> And storm, and darkness, ye are wondrous strong,
> Yet lovely in your strength. —III, xcii.

> Sky, mountains, river, winds, lake, lightnings! ye!
> With night, and clouds, and thunder, and a soul
> To make these felt and feeling, well may be
> Things that have made me watchful. —III, xcvi.

In the last citation we have in a nutshell the phases of the external world that appealed most strongly to Byron. They indicate his love for mystery and darkness, his "fierce and far delight" (*Childe*, III, xciii) in the vast, the somber, and the passionate aspects and moods of Nature.

Byron's Nature-coloring, then, follows the lines of his general interest in being applied to large surfaces, in giving the preference to deep, dark shades, and in seeking twilight and night effects. The preference for dark hues is peculiarly characteristic of Byron, as characteristic as the love of high-lights is of Wordsworth. Blacks, Browns, Purples, and Reds form more than half of his vocabulary, and his other hues are frequently darkened, the better to suit his taste. Thus he has "dark green," "deep green," "dull green," "dusky green,"."sea green," "dark blue," "deep blue," and "dark gray;" and even hues already rich and deep he likes to intensify by throwing them into compounds like "swarthy blush," "purple hectic," "deepest purple," "death-black."

Byron's color effects at night form but a small part of his color as a whole, but they merit notice because of their unusual nature. Twice in *Cain* the purple of the night sky is mentioned. Adah describes Lucifer as

> Like an ethereal night, where long white clouds
> Streak the deep purple.   —*Cain*, I, i, 508–9.

And Cain, as he journeys through space, speaks of

> The very blue of the empurpled night   (II, i, 179),

and again of

> The deep blue noon of night.   —II, ii, 254.

In *Childe Harold* (IV, cxviii) "purple midnight" occurs, and in the *Siege of Corinth* a complete night scene is painted in colors:

> 'Tis midnight : on the mountains brown
> The cold round moon shines deeply down ;
> Blue roll the waters, blue the sky
> Spreads like an ocean, hung on high.
> *   *   *   *   *   *   *

> The waves on either shore lay there
> Calm, clear, and azure as the air.   —*Corinth*, 242.

The explanation of such coloring as this is found in the habits of Byron's daytime brush, rather than in his careful study of unusual effects in Nature.

In fact, despite Byron's protestations as to his love of Nature, a study of his verse, and of the color-treatment in his verse, proves that the poet's professions and his practice were two quite different things: While he says

> I live not in myself, but I become
> Portion of that around me, and to me
> High mountains are a feeling, but the hum
> Of human cities torture,   (*Childe*, III, lxxii),

he really devotes 65 per cent. of his color to Man and abstractions, and it is only in the *Childe Harold* and in passages where he depicts the ocean,

> Dark-heaving, boundless, endless, and sublime,
> The image of Eternity, the throne
> Of the Invisible,   (*Childe*, IV, clxxxii),

that his Nature-hues equal those expended on human beings. Nor does this field of human color-treatment develop, in the sense in which Wordsworth's study of Nature was progressive and developing. Rather Byron's color is frittered away in his latest work on details of dress and ornament, expended, with a childish or oriental delight in gay hues, on descriptions of furniture and costume. No better example of this can be offered than *Don Juan*, III, lxiv–lxxvii, where a whole vocabulary of bright and heterogeneous color is expended upon the garb and surroundings of Juan and Haidee.

Moreover, after his banishment from England Byron's use of colors, like the general tone of his verse, becomes reckless as it becomes more prodigal, is employed more and more as an accessory to sensuous or even sensual pleasure. This is pre-eminently true of *Don Juan*. The *Cain* and the *Heaven and Earth*, both dramatic in character, while far more elevated in tone, are at the same time rather sparing of color. In fact, these two "mysteries" and the *Hebrew Melodies* prove to a striking degree how well Byron, if he chose, could tune his instrument to a lofty religious note. The production, at dates so near together, of *Don Juan* and of *Cain* shows distinctly the dual nature of their author, shows the range of passion which extended from the *Destruction of Sennacherib*, with its effective, emphatic color-touches dropped along the sweep of a picture drawn apparently by a triumphant religious enthusiast, to the bitter frivolity and sensual voluptuousness with which Byron depicts one of the frail beauties of *Don Juan*. And, again, the last cantos of *Childe Harold* were written almost simultaneously with the opening portions of *Don Juan;* the finest of his Nature work, therefore, at the same time with the most sensual, debased, and thoroughly animal of all his productions.

In Byron's best poems, those written after the awakening produced in his mind by foreign travel, and comparatively free from the reckless cynicism of his last work, his color-treatment, while evincing no particular originality of perception or beauty of treatment, is yet liberal, fairly truthful, and generally healthy. His predominant interest is in Man, notwithstanding his oft-repeated declarations as to his love for Nature and for wild solitudes. The noteworthy feature of his work, and that which especially sets him apart from contemporary poets, is the fact that, as his color grows more abundant in his preferred field, it becomes more debased in its application ; that, instead of renouncing color, as did Wordsworth, in favor of nobler instruments of Nature-representation, instead of developing a more definite characterization and treatment of color, as did Coleridge, Byron, at the very moment when he had attained mastery of his art and of its tools, chose to employ one of the most efficient of those tools in degrading rather than in elevating the tone of his work.

CHAPTER IX.

SHELLEY'S USE OF COLOR.

Text used: *Works*, Vols. I-IV. Forman edition. 8 vols. Reeves & Turner, 1880.
Number of lines, 30,030.
For vocabulary see p. 110.

Professor Dowden says of Shelley: "Other poets have more faithfully represented the concrete facts of the world, the characters of many men, the infinite variety of human passions. No other poet has pursued with such breathless speed, on such aerial heights, the spirit of ideal beauty " (*loc. cit.*, p. 17). This statement is not only true of Shelley's poetry as a whole, but also eminently true of his color, which seldom connects itself with concrete objects, but is aërial, ideal, beautiful, breathlessly swift in its progressions and transmutations.

Wordsworth chid himself for his youthful love of "the meagre novelties of form and colour " and turned from these to commune with the more " latent qualities and hidden essences of things " (p. 56). But Shelley, instead of finding color an external, superficial quality of objects, saw it palpitating at the very heart of things — fluid, changing, "immovably unquiet " (*Ode to Liberty*, 78). As day dawns,

> in a fleece of snow-like air,
> The crimson pulse of living morning quivers.
> —*Epips.*, 99–100.

As day dies, the mountain peaks are rendered transparent by

> The inmost spirit of purple light.   —*Julian*, 84.

A beautiful dream-creature is depicted with wings

> Tipt with the speed of liquid lightenings,
> Dyed in the ardours of the atmosphere.
> —*Atlas*, XXXVII.

As the frail Lionel grew day by day weaker,

> the light which flashed through his waxen cheek
> Grew faint, as the rose-like hues which flow
> From sunset o'er the Alpine snow.   —*Rosalind*, 1009-11.

The universe is filled with

> sapphire floods of interstellar air.
> > —*Hellas*, 770.

The hues Shelley loved are everywhere moving, pulsing, changing. They are spirits of the mist, as fleeting and beautiful as the tremulous surface of the soap-bubble. The dewdrop, as it goes through its cycle of being, is but the incarnate spirit of Shelley's coloring —

> A half infrozen dew-globe, green, and gold,
> And crystalline, till it becomes a winged mist
> And wanders up the vault of the blue day,
> Outlives the noon, and on the sun's last ray
> Hangs o'er the sea, a fleece of fire and amethyst.
> > —*Prom.*, IV, 432.

So near to the heart of things does color seem to Shelley that he has connected it with life itself, which,

> like a dome of many-coloured glass,
> Stains the white radiance of Eternity.
> > —*Adonais*, LII.

Yet with all the charm that color had for Shelley's eye, we have no evidence in his verse that it spoke to him of anything higher than beauty. The difference between his attitude and Wordsworth's does not lie in the fact that Shelley found in sensuous impressions what Wordsworth failed to find there. Wordsworth saw the beauty, but this did not satisfy him. His soul longed for a communion with the divine soul of things, which he reached more fully through other channels. Shelley, however, was satisfied with the contemplation of beauty itself. To this he had consecrated himself (see *Hymn to Intellectual Beauty*), and in the enjoyment and pursuit of this he spent his powers of mind and soul. To him beauty was its own excuse for being, and he sought no interpretation of it.

To understand Shelley's coloring it will not be necessary to consider his youthful work apart from that of his maturity, as it is helpful to do in the case of Pope, or Wordsworth, or Byron. Shelley, the poet of "splendours and glooms and glimmering incarnations," singer of "the deep air's unmeasured wildernesses," with its "untameable herds, meteors and mists," seems to have been born fully equipped as a colorist, and to have had Iris as his messenger from the first.

My study of Shelley does not go to support Mr. Havelock Ellis's statement that, "Unlike most . . . . poets he began with no special love of colour, but developed it with his general development" (*loc. cit.*, 721). On the contrary, I have found his youthful poems even richer in color than his later, so that the color-average of *Queen Mab, Alastor*, and *The Revolt of Islam* rises to 56 words per 1,000 lines, whereas the average of his work as a whole is but 48 words (Table II).

In spite, however, of this somewhat greater wealth of color in the verse of his earlier years, I have found it best to consider the salient features of his color as a whole, because his range of hues and his manner of using them are essentially the same throughout his brief life. These salient characteristics, the chief of which I have already mentioned, are ideality, beauty, evanescence, translucence, and a preference for the visionary and unsubstantial rather than for the concrete.

The percentages stated in Table VII give a very imperfect notion of the overwhelming amount of creative and imaginative coloring in Shelley's verse. Under the division Man I have constantly included all visionary creatures and abstractions personified as human beings; and in the realistic work of most of the poets here considered this classification has been quite accurate enough. Spenser's personages or Milton's may with justice be considered as human beings, but such is not the case with Shelley's. Even a real flesh and blood woman like Emilia Viviani becomes to his imagination a creature etherealized, moving about in worlds unrealized — a "Veiled Glory of this lampless universe" (*Epips.*, 26). It is impossible in studying Shelley's verse to distinguish between the real and the imaginary, the human and the super-

human.   When the table shows us a percentage of about one-
fourth of Shelley's total color-interest devoted to Man, this
means a much smaller actual amount, since the bulk of his color-
instances in that field are applied to the ideal, skyey creatures
of his imagination, the

> lovely apparitions, dim at first,
> Then radiant, as the mind, arising bright
> From the embrace of beauty, whence the forms
> Of which these are the phantoms, casts on them
> The gathered rays which are reality.
>
> —*Prom.*, III, iii, 49 ff.

The same is true in the world of Nature.   Actual observation and
study is at a minimum with Shelley.   Professor Dowden (*loc. cit.*,
182) says of him that his shorter studies of Nature are inspira-
tions rather than transcriptions, and this we are ready to believe
when we read of "bloomy spring's star-bright investiture" (*Islam*,
IV, xxxii), or of "the Æolian music" of the sunlight's "sea-green
plumes winnowing the crimson dawn" (*Prom.*, II, i, 26).

We do not, however, lack for real Nature—"the orange light
of widening morn" (*Prom.*, II, i, 18), "lines of gold, hung on
the ashen clouds" (*Sunset*, 13) after sunset, "the blue noon's
burning sky" (*Sunset*, 3), "day's ruddy light" seen through the
delicate hand of an invalid (*Sunset*, 42), a hill seen "hoary
through the white electric rain" (*M. Gisborne*, 124), "weeds like
branching chrysolite" (*Rosalind*, 1083)—, although most of Shelley's realities are in the distance or in the shifting sky.

But in spite of these touches of realistic beauty, the predominant color-effects of Shelley's verse are those of a dream Nature,
a "series of lyric pictures" wherein the figures are of indistinct
and visionary delineation (see *Preface to Hellas*).

It follows naturally from the above that Shelley is a poet of
the ideal rather than of the real, of the delicate and beautiful
rather than of the commonplace.   His hues are used for beauty,
the only ones employed with unpleasant intent being "black,"
"blanched," "bleached," "brimstone," "lurid," "livid," "livid-
blue," "pitchy," "swart," "red" (of bloodshed), and "yellow"
(used of death, death-spasms, a Jew, jealousy, the livery of Peter

Bell, etc.). Otherwise color is for Shelley almost invariably a giver of delight. His pages reveal to us many delicate and unusual hues — "amethystine," "dawn-tinted," "rose-ensanguined," "deep red gold," "moonlight coloured," "chrysolite," — as well as many beautiful color-similes containing comparisons to objects that never had existence outside the poet's brain. For such similes see *Euganean Hills*, 286 ff.; *Alastor*, 433 ff.; *Atlas*, XX, XXXIX, LVII; *Prom.*, IV, 205–35; *Sensitive Plant*, III, 26.

Still, Shelley uses in the main the commoner color-words, enhancing their beauty by his manner of using them, for he is skilled in making "strange combinations out of common things": "blue oceans of young air" (*Epips.*, 460), "smoke wool-white as ocean foam" (*Rosalind*, 1092), "the azure time of June" (*Rosalind*, 957).

That which is markedly peculiar to Shelley in his application of color is the varying evanescent pulsation which he seems to see, and to delight to see, in all bright hues. Especially is this true when he is observing or creating atmospheric effects: "rainbow-skirted showers," "liquid mists of splendour," "light on a careering stream of golden clouds,"

> That Light whose smile kindles the Universe,
> That Beauty in which all things live and move.
> — *Adonais*, LIV.

Into Shelley's color

> A maze of light and life and motion
> Is woven.   —*Rosalind*, 129–30.

Indeed the very word "woven" had for him a charm. This and its related forms "weave," "wove," and "woof," with such kindred words as "braided," "intertwined," "intertangled," etc., he repeatedly applies to the insubstantial fabric of light and mist, of sound and odor and hue. Mr. Havelock Ellis has called attention to this fact, as well as to Shelley's admiration of fire, that embodiment of "life and light and motion." The two preferences just named may be advantageously studied in *The Witch of Atlas*. In fact, Shelley's art as a poet-painter closely resembles that of the *Witch* herself, who

took her spindle,
And twined three threads of fleecy mist, and three
Long lines of light, such as the dawn may kindle
The clouds and mountains with, and she
As many star-beams, ere their lamp could dwindle
In the belated moon, wound skilfully;
And with these threads a subtle veil she wove,
A shadow for the splendour of her love.

— *Witch*, XIII.

A soul of such loves and such powers will naturally become the poet of an extra-mundane universe. Such is Shelley. Subtle robe of mist and splendor and "sinuous veil of woven wind" are not the clothing of everyday people in an everyday world ; they are suited only to radiant creations of the fancy. Nor does "light dissolved in star showers" shine upon Regent Street and the Strand. If Shelley's feet did touch the earth, his eyes were upon the "emerald main," the "misty mountains, wide and vast," and the "azure heaven." There he built up his visionary universe, "Obedient to the light that shone within his soul." There he placed each "shape of speechless beauty" spun "from the fine threads of rare and subtle thought," and there we may see his most beautiful coloring and most delicate effects of light and shade.

Such a passage as that cited below exhibits in combination all the characteristics which I have mentioned as belonging to Shelley's color as a whole — its ideality, its beauty, its translucence, its pulsating life, its unsubstantiality, and its evanescence :

The point of one white star is quivering still
Deep in the orange light of widening morn
Beyond the purple mountains : through a chasm
Of wind-divided mist the darker lake
Reflects it : now it wanes : it gleams again
As the waves fade, and as the burning threads
Of woven cloud unravel in the pale air :
'Tis lost ! and through yon peaks of cloudlike snow
The roseate sunlight quivers : hear I not
The Æolian music of her sea-green plumes
Winnowing the crimson dawn ?   — *Prom.*, II, i, 17–27.

Shelley's color-sense was full and well balanced. He was a master in every line of hues and used all without any noteworthy limitations of partiality. His vocabulary of bright hues is made up of cold and warm tones in about equal proportions, though he uses Greens and Blues more than he does Reds and Yellows. He falls below the poetic average in Reds, Greens, and Blacks, but rises above it in Blues, Grays, and Golds.

In the distribution of his colors, however, Shelley does not show the impartiality that he does in their choice. He manifests an overwhelming preference for atmospheric and skyey phenomena, for "pageantry of mists," and "the varying roof of heaven." An hour's reading of his verse will demonstrate this as conclusively as a page of quotations.

Other sense-preferences than that for light and color are also marked in Shelley's verse. The student of his hues cannot fail to notice his frequent mention of odors and his keen enjoyment of them. No other poet here considered comes anywhere near Shelley in the number of his references to the sense of smell. Cowper indeed possesses an enjoyment of odors, but he does not mention them with frequency. Shelley found the odors of musk-rose and jasmine "soul-dissolving." Blooming myrtle and lemon flowers scattered for him a "sense-dissolving fragrance." When the warm wind shook the fresh green leaves of the sweet briar,

> there were odours then to make
> The very breath we did respire
> A liquid element, whereon
> Our spirits, like delighted things
> That walk the air on subtle wings,
> Floated and mingled far away
> ' Mid the warm winds of the sunny day.
> — *Rosalind*, 961-7.

Violets and jonquils

> dart their arrowy odour through the brain
> Till you might faint with that delicious pain.
> — *Epips.*, 451-2.

Sometimes, as if language failed him for direct description of odors, he tries to define them in terms of another sense :

> flowers of gentle breath,
> Like incarnations of the stars, when splendour
> Is changed to fragrance.
> — *Adonais*, XX.

> In that star's smile, whose light is like the scent
> Of a jonquil when evening breezes fan it.
> — *Triumph*, 419-20.

> And soon her strain
> The nightingale began, ...
>
> *   *   *   *   *   *   *
>
> And now to the hushed ear it floats
> Like field smells known in infancy.
> — *Rosalind*, 1104-10.

The last citation affords an interesting point of comparison between Shelley and one or two other English poets. Cowper, describing himself as a very little child, mentions especially the fact that he wore a "scarlet mantle" (*Mother's Picture*, 51). Color evidently made a keen impression on his baby-mind. Coleridge also, in his *Sonnet to the River Otter*, refers to the "sweet scenes of childhood" as recurring to him always with a picture of the river's tints, the "marge with willows gray," and the bedded sand that gleamed with "various dyes." Wordsworth, too, recalls a river, but for its sound that "blended with his nurse's song" (*Prel.*, I, 271). But it would seem that Shelley, in the passage last quoted from him, connects his early recollections with the sense of smell, that sense which, though dull in comparison with some others, has yet the strongest associative memory.

Shelley's sense of sound is keen also, developed to the highest degree and treated with the same luxuriance of imaginative enjoyment that everywhere characterizes his thought. But I speak particularly of his susceptibility to odors as being a marked idiosyncracy of his verse, an idiosyncracy found in no other poet here studied.

From all the data here given, we draw conclusions as to Shelley's color agreeing with the general truths sketched by Professor Dowden in the quotation that begins this chapter, and by Mr. Masson (*loc. cit.*, p. 140), when he speaks of the remoteness of

Shelley's thought from terrestrial conditions. We can even see the tendencies of Shelley's color-work reflected in the panorama of his brilliant, restless, sensitive life. His intense craving for liberty and freedom—can we not parallel this with the spaces of the heavens, the depths of interstellar air, in which Shelley's mind loved to expand its buoyant wings? Can we not liken the beauty and the ideality of his painting to the high-thoughted impulses which guided his headlong flight towards what he believed was truth, believed was sublimity? And surely the evanescent glory of his poetry finds its counterpart in the brief bright life which shone out for a few unparalleled years and then went suddenly down into darkness, leaving its line of light traveling toward the earth, to reach it only long after the star was quenched.

CHAPTER X.

KEATS'S USE OF COLOR.

Text used : *Works*, Vols. I and II. Forman edition. 4 vols. Reeves &
Turner, 1883.
Number of lines, 13,991.
For vocabulary see pp. 110-11.

By literary critics the wealth of color in the verse of Keats
has long been acknowledged. And even the casual reader of
his poetry has been strongly attracted by the richness and delicacy
of such pictures as that of the chamber of "St. Agnes' charmed
maid":

> A casement high and triple-arch'd there was,
> All garlanded with carven imageries
> Of fruits and flowers, and bunches of knot-grass,
> And diamonded with panes of quaint device,
> Innumerable of stains and splendid dyes,
> As are the tiger-moth's deep-damask'd wings ;
> And in their midst, 'mong thousand heraldries,
> And twilight saints, and dim emblazonings,
> A shielded scutcheon blush'd with blood of queens and kings.
>
> Full on this casement shone the wintry moon,
> And threw warm gules on Madeline's fair breast,
> As down she knelt for heaven's grace and boon ;
> Rose-bloom fell on her hands, together prest,
> And on her silver cross soft amethyst,
> And on her hair a glory, like a saint :
> She seemed a splendid angel, newly drest,
> Save wings, for heaven : — Porphyro grew faint :
> She knelt, so pure a thing, so free from mortal taint.
>
> —*The Eve of St. Agnes*, XXIV–XXV.

Here we have the delicacy of Shelley united with Spenser's
wealth of suggestion : not only has the poet put in loving touches

of actual color, rare and beautiful—"rose-bloom," "soft amethyst" falling over "silver," "warm gules," "deep-damask"—but
he has accompanied these by a richness and splendor of suggestion that stimulate to the full the æsthetic sense, and he has
infused into them a throbbing life.

The Eve of St. Agnes was one of the later works of the
young poet who first tried his pen in imitating the stanzas of
Spenser. Keats's career was short and intense, for death claimed
him when he was less than twenty-six years of age ; but in the
brief term of his literary productiveness he passed through many
phases of poetic experience, phases whose extremes are to some
extent recorded in the colors which he used and the manner in
which he used them.

His poetry, as a whole, is flooded with light and color, though
the distribution of these varies greatly. Sometimes he loses himself in a maze of luxuriant imagery, his youthful, effervescent
emotion delighting in displays of Asiatic brilliancy : we are sur-
feited with dazzle and gorgeous hues. The dream palaces of
Endymion are cases in point. But at other times he displays a
remarkable power of withholding color altogether from a poem,
as in La Belle Dame Sans Merci, or of so controlling and har-
monizing his tints that they are introduced into the picture
only where they contribute to high æsthetic delight ; for example,
in The Eve of St. Agnes, and in the St. Mark fragments that so
deeply impressed Rossetti and his pre-Raphaelite brethren, the
hues are abundant and vivid, but always under the control of a
disciplined imagination and a perfect artistic taste.

This variety in modes of color-treatment seems to arise from
two sets of forces, the one connected with Keats's maturing
tastes and powers of mind, and with the partial calming of his
youthful emotions, the other growing out of his extraordinary
instinct for keeping his poetic style in harmony with his theme.

To realize the change which took place in him between 1812
and 1820 we may compare his first poem, Stanzas in Imitation of
Spenser, and his last sonnet, Bright Star! Would I were Steadfast
as Thou art. In the thirty-six lines of the former there are,
fourteen direct color-terms—"verdant," "amber," "silvering,"

" golden," "ruby," "snow," "jetty," "ebony," "emeràld," "silver,"
"white," "cærulean," "verdure," and "ruddy," several of which
are quite as full of sheen as of hue. There are also seven phrases
more or less clearly hinting color: "mossy beds," "beds of
simple flowers," "reflected woven bowers," "plumage bright,"
"brilliant dye," "the flowery side" of a stream, "all the buds in
Flora's diadem." If now we add to these the terms that express
a shine and sheen—"flame," "silken," "sparkled," "sheen,"
"glossy," "bright," "glow"—we have some thirty light and
color appeals to the eye in thirty-six lines. The effect is one
of unpruned richness and glow. The hues are not only varied
and vivid, but enameled.

Now contrast with this Keats's last tender and beautiful
sonnet. The warmth of color seen in his earliest verse has here
given place to a tender twilight glory. · He puts into his picture
now only the brightness of the steadfast star, the far-off shine of
priestlike waters, and the gleam of a "new, soft-fallen mask
of snow."

A somewhat similar result is obtained by comparing the long
poems that stand, broadly speaking, for the two phases of his
work, the *Endymion* and the *Hyperion*. The former has a complete range of colors,[1] and an incalculable amount of sunlight
and moonlight splendors, spangle and diamond light, massed
with luxuriant and emotional effect. The latter has few bright
colors,[2] and these are nowhere massed. Its emphasis is put
upon Whites, particularly Whites kindled with shining light. See,
for example, the description of the aged Saturn :

> And in each face he saw a gleam of light,
> But splendider in Saturn's, whose hoar locks
> Shone like the bubbling foam about a keel
> When the prow sweeps into a midnight cove.
>
> *Hyperion,* II, 352–5.

Again, if we compare the bright hues on Keats's early palette
with those found oftenest on his later, still another difference

[1] Reds 24, Yellows 39, Blues 28, Greens 38, Purples 4, Browns 4, Whites
81, Grays 3, Blacks 20.
[2] Reds 9, Yellows 8, Greens 5, Brown 1, Whites 26, Grays 3, Blacks 8.

between his two manners as a colorist will come to light. Seven-
tenths of all his Yellows and more than half of his Reds belong
to that period of "yeasting youth" (*Otho*, III, ii, 178) when he
wrote the *Poems of 1817* and *Endymion;* but both his Greens and
his Blues strike an about even balance in the two periods, in spite
of the latter's absence from *Hyperion*. We may therefore conclude
that while the warm, luminous colors attracted Keats in his youth,
the calmer colors-yielded him a more steady and permanent
satisfaction. The boy Keats must have been like the youthful
Carlyle, a bit of whose biography comes to us through the
mouth of Teufelsdröckh :

> On fine summer evenings I was wont to carry forth my supper
> (bread crumb boiled in milk) and eat it out of doors. On the coping
> of the Orchard wall . . . . my porringer was placed ; there, many a
> sunset, have I, looking on the distant western Mountains, consumed,
> not without relish, my evening meal. Those hues of gold and azure,
> that hush of World's expectation as Day died, were still a Hebrew
> Speech to me ; nevertheless I was looking at the fair, illuminated
> Letters, and had an eye to their gilding. (*Sartor Resartus*, II, chap. 2.)

Keats, too, had "an eye for the gilding," in common with
youthful poets in general, and in the *Endymion* he applied this
gilding to a remarkable degree.

These, then, are the tendencies established by the first set
of forces which I mentioned, the forces connected with his
gradually maturing tastes and powers: a lessening emphasis
upon warm, vivid hues, a strengthening love for cool, calm hues,
and withal a steady, persistent affection for bright light,
especially—as was fitting in our "moon-poet"—for silvery
moonlight effects.

The second set of forces that tend to influence his choice of
colors in particular poems arises, as I have said, from the power
which he had of putting himself instinctively into sympathy with
his theme. He could sketch in what Sidney Colvin calls "his
own rich and decorated English way" (*loc. cit.*, p. 153), laying
in his colors with artless lavishness, as in *Calidore* and *I stood
tiptoe;* he could portray in appropriate heraldic hues such a
unique pre-Raphaelite figure as that of Bertha in *The Eve of St.*

Mark; or he could use the alphabet of classic color in telling us the story of the early gods, as in *Hyperion.* It is here, in the *Hyperion,* that his instinctive adaptation to the Greek spirit comes out most strongly. It is found also in *To Autumn* and *On a Grecian Urn.* In these poems there is a striking likeness between his range of color-terms and that pointed out by Mr. Gladstone as found in Homer (*loc. cit.,* pp. 382–8). Here are no Blues and Violets; white predominates, yellow and red are used occasionally, green appears, but receives very slight notice.

Reference to Tables III and V will show that by the majority of the poets there represented Whites are used oftener than any other line of hues. Keats, then, is by no means peculiar in having Whites at the head of his list; and yet one who studies his use of these feels that they were particularly attractive to him and depicted by him with loving relish. The reason for this seems to me to lie in the intensity of his sensuous endowment. His was a soul "all passion struck " (*Faery,* II, 9). He possessed senses so exquisitely refined that their gratification gave him both ecstatic pleasure and ecstatic pain. His nerves were all a-tingle to the delights of the world, and he describes for us such a range of sense-enjoyments as would be hard to parallel. In significant accord, therefore, with the fullness of his sensuous nature, is his passionate enjoyment of white light, the radiance of the uncolored beam of sunlight, strongest among visual stimulants.

The number of words expressing dazzle and sheen is very large in Keats's verse : " bright," " shining," " gleaming," " glistening," " glossy," " lustrous," " lucid," " luminous," " crystal," " spangly," " phosphor," " diamond," etc., etc. When these cannot meet his need, he intensifies them in the most superlative way : " passionately bright " (*End.,* I, 594), " bright enough to drive me mad " (*End.,* I, 613). He seems to connect with them, not only excessive visual stimulation, but an emotional rapture as well, as when once he speaks of

Touching with dazzled lips her starlight hand.

—*End.,* IV, 419.

Next to glow and luster in the list of Keats's pleasures of sight
come Whites, which are frequently luminous. He likes them
alone, and he also makes especially felicitous combinations of
his Whites with other delicate hues, as in the lines —

> Here are sweet peas, on tiptoe for a flight,
> With wings of gentle flush o'er delicate white
>
> (I stood tiptoe, 57-8),

or in lines 8–10 and 113–15 of the poem just cited, where
he introduces a combination peculiarly pleasing to him — white
clouds and blue sky. Such a scene he speaks of in a letter to
Jane Reynolds, 1817, as " fulfilling " to him.

Keats indulges freely in the ordinary Whites of ballad figure-
painting : the women, real or ideal, whom he worships have
"ivory" wrist, and neck, and breast, "milk-white" shoulders,
"lily" hands, "marble" arms. But such trite poetizing he can
far transcend, as when, with loving admiration and artistic touch,
he clothes Madeline

> In blanchèd linen smooth and lavendered
>
> (St. Agnes, XXX);

or pictures Apollo's "white melodious throat" (*Hyp.*, III, 81) ;
or dreams how

> Young buds sleep in the root's white core
>
> (Faery, 1, 4);

or causes Endymion to name among the delights with which he
will make happy his Indian Princess,

> I will entice this crystal rill to trace
> Love's silver name upon the meadow's face.
>
> —End., IV, 699.

Gray is used very little by Keats ; it has a predominant association with old age, and enters into none of his creative pictures,
unless we may count the line in his sonnet *Blue*,

> The bosomer of clouds, grey, gold, and dun.

Black also is sparingly employed in Keats's verse, and when
it does appear it is usually in passages where the color-idea is
subordinate to some more important idea, or where the dark
shade is mentioned merely as a foil for some lighter one.

Reds he seemed to prize and use chiefly for their association
with the English flowers and fruits that he loved, with the splendors of dawn or of sunset, and with the glow of health or the
play of emotion in the human countenance. For one red hue he
cherished great repugnance — for the pungent scarlet. Perhaps
the association with the uniform of the English soldier destroyed
any æsthetic pleasure that he might otherwise have had for the
hue. It is seldom, however, a favorite with poets. Like its
crude sister, orange, it suffers neglect at their hands. When
Keats lay stretched on the grass with a field of drooping oats on
the one side, and on the other

> Ocean's blue mantle streaked with purple and green,

he was annoyed by the upstart poppies,

> So pert and useless that they bring to mind
> The scarlet coats that pester humankind.
> > —*Epistle to my Brother George*, 129 ff.

When the serpent Lamia underwent her torture of transforma-
tion,

> She writhed about, convulsed with scarlet pain
> > (*Lamia*, I, 154),

and once Endymion, in an oppressive dream, saw with horror
that

> ̗ the vermeil rose had blown
> In frightful scarlet.   —*End.*, I, 696.

Avoiding, then, the more intense red, and especially that
admixed with orange, Keats prefers the softer red, modified by
an admixture of white. For his most beautiful touches of rich
color he chooses " bloom," " flush," " blush," and " rose," as in
the following lines :

> The creeper, mellowing with an autumn blush.
> > —*End.*, II, 416.

> While barred clouds bloom the soft-dying day
> And touch the stubble-plains with rosy hue.
> > —*Autumn*, 25.

> Smooth semilucent mist
> Diversely tinged with rose and amethyst.
> > —*End.*, IV, 386.

> At five the golden light began to spring
> With fiery shudder through the bloomèd east.
> > —*Cap and Bells*, LXXX.

The last citation reminds one of Shelley, who loved to paint the tints that quiver upon

> The vaporous spray
> Which the sun clothes in hues of Iris light.
> > —*Orpheus*, 80.

But the imagination of Keats is, on the whole, less ethereal than that of Shelley. His objects are more concrete and graspable, and his coloring is more opaque. This may be seen in his Yellows, where the gold — his favorite yellow — is less translucent than Shelley's translucent gold. They are more solid and metallic, reminding one of the gold grounds of Fra Angelico.

In Table III we see that in the amount of his yellow Keats is surpassed by Spenser only. His high percentage here is due to his "gold," which constitutes four-fifths of all his yellow. Next to this he likes best "amber," which has brilliancy as used in his verse, and for this reason ranks next to the merry-shining "gold."

Another noticeable thing in Keats's percentages, as shown in Table III, is the equal amounts of red, of yellow, and of green. As I have before said, the largest part of his Yellows occur in the *Poems of 1817* and *Endymion*. But with his Greens the case is different. In these he seems to take increasing pleasure as time goes on. The highest color-pleasure of his last years came from the hues of the great physical wholes — green fields, blue sea and sky. These hues rested and soothed him, contributing a tranquillizing calm to his passionate emotional nature. Even his early poems furnish lines to which one may point as confirmation of this (*e. g.*, *Calidore*, 1–10). And if in his later work the calming effect of the green is less directly expressed, we still feel the subtle joy which the poet takes in its cool restfulness, in poems like *To a Nightingale*.

Blue is not numerically predominant in Keats's verse, but no one who reads his sonnet answering the one which J. H. Reynolds had written in praise of dark eyes, as

dearer far
Than those which mock the hyacinthine bell,

can doubt that blue gave Keats æsthetic satisfaction, or that it
had not for him distinct association with the things most dear to
him — the expanse of heaven, "bosomer of clouds," the sweet
English flowers, and the human eyes whose blue he felt "run
liquid" through his soul (*End.*, II, 543).

Throughout his life Keats was a worshiper of beauty. At
first the ideal good seems to have assumed for him a form more
or less material. At the time when he wrote

A thing of beauty is a joy forever   (*End.*, I, 1),

his eager nature found satisfaction in luxuriant imagery of cloy-
ing sweetness, or in the excessive gratification of personal sensa-
tion ; but his worship was too sincere, his sympathies were too
high, for him long to follow the goddess afar off. His insight
became more spiritual, his expression less decorative and more
noble, as he approached the period when he gave utterance to
the exquisite ode *On a Grecian Urn.* There he proclaims,

Beauty is truth, truth beauty ;

and in a letter of 1817 :

I am certain of nothing but of the holiness of the heart's affections
and the truth of imagination. What the imagination seizes as beauty
must be truth, whether it existed before or not ; for I have the same
idea of all the passions as of love ; they are all, in their sublime, creative of essential beauty. (Letter to Benj. Bailey, November 22, 1817.)

And again he wrote :

You speak of Lord Byron and me. There is this great difference
between us: he describes what he sees, I describe what I imagine. (To
George Keats, July 26, 1818.)

These utterances are of large significance to the interpreter
of Keats's poetry. In studying his coloring we should remember
that the scenes of his poems are laid not so often in the English
district where he wrote, as in the land of his imagination, where
the lights and shades, the hues and tints, are not so truly what
he saw in Nature as what he delighted to see. To test Keats's

coloring by his own criterion, the reader must ask, not "Is this faithful to reality?", but "Does this present to the quickened imagination a picture of 'essential beauty'?" Tried by this test, the "rose-bloom" and "amethyst" cast by the moonbeams upon fair Madeline will forever remain things of beauty in spite of the fact that colors are not so cast at night. And the gorgeous array of colors adorning Lamia, that

> Gordian shape of dazzling hue,
> Vermilion-spotted, golden, green, and blue,
> Striped like a zebra, freckled like a pard,
> Eyed like a peacock, and all crimson barr'd
>
> (*Lamia*, I, 47),

though never was there a serpent so clothed, will continue to surprise many a reader into admiration.

For exquisite truth in rendering Nature's sounds and colors we should go to Wordsworth, or Tennyson, or Browning; but Keats's mission, like Shelley's, was to create. "The points of leaves and twigs on which the spider begins work," he once wrote, "are few, and she fills the air with a beautiful circuiting. Man should be as content with as few points to tip with the fine web of his soul and weave a tapestry empyrean — full of symbols for his spiritual eye, of space for his wanderings, of distinctness for his luxury." (To *Reynolds*, February 19, 1818.) The colors in which Keats wove his "tapestry empyrean" are strong and definite, whether they dazzle or soothe us. If he seemed to possess a dual color-taste — now reveling in the brightest, most luminous rays of light, and now turning for "calmness" to the more tranquil Blues and verdure tints — he was in both consistent. His passionate nature led him to marshal the intense Reds and Golds and dazzling Whites until he was ready to swoon, intoxicated by their refulgence; but when he had taken his draught of sunshine, he experienced conscious joy in the contemplation of the softer complementaries of these gorgeous hues, and in restful twilight gleams.

His colors were not conventional like those of Pope. If in large measure ideal, they were never artificial. They were not the evanescent, etherealized hues of Shelley, but had body and a

steady glow. As compared with Wordsworth's colors founded
upon close observation of Nature and of life, Keats's show
broader effects and less careful discriminations. In the extent of
his vocabulary he falls short of the three poets especially distin-
guished as human colorists—Shakspere, Scott, and Byron ; but
where their color-averages are respectively 12, 48, and 25 words
per 1,000 lines, Keats's average rises to 65 words. In wealth
of color he stands without a peer.

CONCLUSION.

The general conclusions which we may draw from the fore-going facts and from different classifications of our figures may be stated under three heads : I, Color-Vocabulary ; II, Color Scale ; III, Color-Distribution. The vocabulary lists, tables, and charts that are concerned with these divisions of our subject are grouped as follows :

I.   COLOR-VOCABULARY.

PAGE

Classified vocabularies of the seventeen poets here studied, arranged chronologically, - - - - - - 103
A comparative vocabulary of Elizabethan color and Romantic color, - - - - - - - - - 111
Table I, giving a numerical summary of the number of variants used by different poets, - - - - - - 114

II.   COLOR-SCALE.

Table II, showing the actual number of times each poet uses each color-group, the number of lines catalogued for each, and the color-average for each per 1,000 lines, - - 115
Table III, showing the percentage of color falling in each color-group (based on the figures of II), and the relative proportions of definite and indefinite hues used by each poet, - 115
Table IV, listing for each poet the ten color-words oftenest used, 116
Table V, showing each poet's color-scale, and that of the Romanticists as a body, according to color-groups, - - 116

III.   COLOR-DISTRIBUTION.

Table VI, showing the actual number of times each poet applies color to the various fields of interest, A-Z (p. 113), - 117
Table VII, showing the percentage of color falling in each field (based on the figures of VI), - - - - - - 117
Table VIII, showing, for the Romanticists as a body, the way in which each of the nine color-groups is distributed through the fields A-Z, - - - - - - - 118

PAGE

Table IX, showing the relative amounts of the different colors in any one of the fields A–Z   -   -   -   -   -   -   118

Chart A, showing the fluctuations of the color-vocabulary applied to Man by the poets from the fourteenth to the nineteenth centuries.

Chart B, showing the growth of the color-vocabulary applied to Nature.

I. POETIC COLOR-VOCABULARY.

From Table I and the vocabulary lists given on pp. 103–12, it will at once appear that there have been two great periods of abundant color-vocabulary in English poetry, from the time of Chaucer to that of Keats—the Elizabethan and the Romantic. A glance at Charts A and B will show the radical difference in application of the two bodies of color. The individual and comparative vocabularies now under consideration indicate other points of distinction between the two ages.

The Elizabethan vocabulary as used by Shakspere and Spenser was strong in Reds, Whites, and Blacks; *i. e.*, in human coloring (Charts A and B show the strongly human application of color in this period). Shakspere's color-vocabulary is the largest of any here studied, Byron's coming next. While Byron's, however, is composed of the *real* colors, and owes its extent possibly to his observance of many nations, Shakspere's abundance of color-terms is due to his exuberant dramatic fancy. He employs such words as " Cain-colored," " French-crown-colored," " orange-tawny," " freestone-colored," " paly ashes," " cold-pale," " maid-pale," etc.

The differentiations of color, *i. e.*, the creation or perception of subvarieties of the chief color, such as "crimson-red," "rose-red," "blood-red," as varieties of red, are in the Elizabethans confined largely to the color-groups which I have already mentioned as the fullest—Reds, Whites, and Blacks; this fact indicates the accuracy and preference with which their object of interest — Man — was studied by them.[1]

---

[1] That these two peculiarities, abundant use of color and differentiation in its shades as used, are not necessarily co-existent, may be seen by a glance at

The Elizabethan vocabulary, then, was distinctly a human one. If we drop from Shakspere's vocabulary those words used exclusively of Nature, we should still have left 104 of his 114 terms, while in Wordsworth's case we should, after a similar subtraction, have remaining only 57 of his 93 words The Romantic vocabulary, on the other hand, though keeping Reds and Whites at the head numerically, was also much developed in the Greens, Blues, Purples, and Browns. The explanation of this retention of red and white is seen by a glance at Charts A and B. The Elizabethan period had but one center of interest — Man ; the Romantic period, while lifting Nature and Nature-study into prominence, did not avert its eyes from humanity; it thus has two centers of interest and two co-existent and nearly equal fields of color-treatment. As exhibited on pp. 111–12, the vocabularies of Spenser and Shakspere together contain 139 color-terms. Of these Elizabethan terms the Romanticists retain 96, and add to these 135, making a total of 231 terms. Of the 43 terms dropped from the earlier color-vocabulary 10 may be counted as now obsolete — *e. g.*, "watchet," "blunket," "gilt" (= red), "auburn" (= yellow), "welkin," "gaudy-green;" another ten are dramatic coinings by Shakspere, struck out for use at the moment — *e. g.*, "cheek-roses," "linen-faced," "tallow-faced," "cold-pale," "nighted," etc.; still others are intensive compounds whose separate words are common poetic property, but whose particular combinations are not found in the work of the Romanticists — *e. g.*, "scarlet-red," "vermeil-red," "raven-black," "pale-white," "orange-tawny." Of these 43 terms 37 were confined in their application to Man and his clothing, showing again the strong bias of Spenser and Shakspere toward human coloring.

If now we look at the additions made to the vocabulary by the Romantic poets, it will appear that among them Nature-hues predominate : the Browns, Greens, and Blues have been doubled ; the Purples raised from 1 to 13. The additions are made in differentiations of staple hues, rather than in the introduction of

Scott's Browns, for example : although he employs only 5 per cent. of brown he recognizes six varieties in its tone.

new root-words, though there are some additions of the latter
class, *e. g.*, "pink," "pomegranate," "flesh-colored," "chrysolite,"
"glaucous," "amethyst," "grain." "lilac," "violet," "bronze,"
"cinereous." The differentiated shades and tints added by the
later school are very numerous. It is a curious fact that the
Elizabethan vocabularies here cited contain only one *shade* in
the proper sense of that word (*i. e.*, the deepening or darkening
of a primary hue). This one shade is Shakspere's "deep-green
emerald." The only Elizabethan tints are "pallid-green,"
"pallid-blue," and "hoary-gray."

Beside this meager list place the Romanticists' shades and tints:
"dark-red," "deep-red," "dull-red," "dusky-red," "dark-blue,"
"dead-blue," "deep-blue," "gloomy-blue," "sable-blue," "black-
blue," "dark-green," "deep-green," "dull-green," "dusky-green,"
"gloomy-green," "sepulchral-green," "dark-brown," "deep-
brown," "dark-purple," "deepest-purple," "pale-blue," "lurid-
blue," "livid-blue," "light-brown," "light-green," "pale-gray,"
"silver-gray," "paly-red," "paly-rose." We have in the two
lists a marked difference of observation, of usage, or of both.

Another contrast we may draw between the compound hues
of the Elizabethans and those of the Romanticists. The former
are either obvious, a part of the common ballad stock of descriptive adjectives—"raven-black," "rose-red," "fiery-red," "milk-
white," "snow-white," etc.—or such as are fanciful and dramatic
—"Cain-colored," "linen-faced," "cheek-roses." Again, if
Spenser or Shakspere combines two color-words into a single
adjective, the two are usually synonyms, and the compound is
intensive rather than discriminating—"crimson-red," "scarlet-
red," "sanguine-red," "pale-white."

The characteristic compounds made by the Romantic School,
on the other hand, combine two different hues in such a way that
one modifies the other. There are coined new color-terms that,
instead of being intensive or dramatic, are discriminative and
æsthetic; such terms as "rubious-argent," "pinky-silver,"
"swarthy-red," "purple-hectic," "dun-red," "purple-gold,"
"ruddy-brown," "yellow-green," "purple-amethyst," "autumnal-
leaf like-red," "gold green," "tawny-green," "deep-red-gold,"

and "rose-ensanguined-ivory." These new compound tones are about equally divided in application between Man and Nature, with a slight leaning to the latter; so that once more we see the double and well-rounded color-interest of the Romantic School, an interest which shows itself this time in conjunction with an increasingly æsthetic handling of color.

To recapitulate, the Elizabethan color-vocabulary contains nearly all the root-words for color that are found in English poetry up to the beginning of the present century, and with the exception of a few terms now obsolete, and a few individual coinings of Shakspere's fancy, it has passed almost undiminished into modern verse. Its strength lies in terms descriptive of Man's face, hair, and dress. The Romantic color-vocabulary, while retaining the majority of the terms of Spenser and Shakspere, adds to these a few new terms, chiefly for delicate and translucent hues — "pomegranate," "amethyst," "violet," "lilac," "chryso-lite," etc. — and then proceeds to mix the old staple hues upon its palette until it has a numerous body of tints, shades, and compound tones, suited to describe æsthetically, not only Man, but Nature, and Nature in both steady and evanescent aspects.

Chart A presents to the eye the variety of hues which different poets have noted in eyes, hair, and skin. Shakspere here outstrips both predecessors and successors. He has 23 adjectives and compounds to express the whiteness or pallor of the skin, 9 for its tones of red and pink, 18 for its Yellows and dark hues. He employs, first, the staple colors and their commoner compounds, such as are found in the ballads. Then he does not hesitate, in addition to these, to coin new words; and some of them are more than mere hues — they are dramatic phrases carrying along with the color-touch a train of deeper suggestion, indicating character. Such, for example, are "linen-faced," "whey-faced," "maid-pale." One feels throughout, in the study of Shakspere, that he was a master in the field of human coloring, and that in characterizing abstract qualities he could wield the brush with a careless mastery to be observed almost nowhere outside his pages.[1] His Nature-hues, however, though true and

[1] Note his percentage in Class Z, Table VII.

beautiful, are limited, as was but natural in lyric and dramatic work whose interest was preponderatingly human.

Spenser, however, had a subject and a method which invited color. It is therefore surprising to find that his color-vocabulary is smaller than Shakspere's, and that in using it he reaches an average of only 15 words per 1,000 lines, less than one-fourth that of Gray and Keats. And yet, because of his generous color-hinting, and his pervading glooms and gleams, he suggests to us Keats, richest of colorists.

After Shakspere's time interest in color wanes. Milton, to be sure, has a coloring pure and dignified, yet it is scanty. Pope, who represents the eighteenth century with a color-vocabulary less copious than Chaucer's, though he uses his terms more frequently than the preceding poets of our tables do, uses them with a connotation which in the majority of instances degrades or minimizes their color-value. With him, after his earliest years of production, hues become the tools of satire and sarcasm.

Such minor writers of the eighteenth century as John Phillips, Richard Savage, John Dyer, and John Scott[1] really observed the hues of Nature, and noticed in their verse tints and shades less obvious than the "green" forest, "blue" sky, and "white" moon with which ballad writers are for the most part content. They thus prepared the way for Thomson, who with direct intent devoted himself in *The Seasons* to the study of the external world. He had not a magic touch, but he gave himself with love to the observation of a genuine Nature, and used in depicting it a color-vocabulary twice as large as that employed by Shakspere in the same field. His color-vocabulary as a whole is the largest between those of Shakspere and the Romanticists. In its Browns and Greens it shows the differentiations characteristic of the latter school. Thomson also reflects in his verse some of the contemporary scientific study of chromatics, for he gives in order the rainbow hues, as classified by the physicists, and again catalogues the same in his lines on the spectrum in *To Newton*.

Gray's vocabulary is small, though lavishly used in his 1,300 lines of verse. Goldsmith is strikingly meager as a colorist,

[1] Reynolds, *loc. cit.*, Index, " Color."

with his fifteen words used in all only twenty-six times. Cowper, too, has a small color-average, though a vocabulary about like that of Spenser and Milton.

It is with Scott, who has a vocabulary surpassed only by Shakspere's and Byron's, full in almost every group of hues, and well-balanced between Man and Nature, that the second great color-wave of English poetry — the wave whose rise we feel in Thomson — approaches its crest. Upon this wave we are carried to the high tide of the great Romantic color-movement.

II. POETIC COLOR-SCALE.

The ratio in which different hues appeal to the human eye, the relative amount of attention which the poet gives them in his verse — these are questions of psychological and æsthetic interest, even though physiologists fail to find in such statistics any definite index to the extent and accuracy of man's vision.

The accompanying tables are not so extensive that they may be considered determinative and final in [their judgment as to the color-scale of English poetry, yet it may be claimed for them that they offer a definite contribution toward such a judgment. Representing as they do thirteen of England's leading poets, poets typical of all the centuries from the fourteenth to the present time, and of all the great literary movements of England ; representing, too, every class of poetic production, from the purely didactic to the purely descriptive, or from the most highly artistic drama to the most spontaneous and personal "lyrical cry"—they should, in their total of nearly half a million lines of verse, furnish us with an approximately truthful poetic color-scale.

Table II shows the actual number of times which each poet uses his Reds, his Yellows, his Greens, etc., with the total number of times color occurs in his verse, the total number of lines catalogued for each poet, and his average number of color-words per 1,000 lines.

Table III is based upon II, but furnishes a readier means of comparing the different poets, because its figures are expressed as percentages. Appended to these percentages, according to the nine color-groups, is a second set of percentages showing the relative proportion of definite and indefinite¹ hues in each poet's verse.

In Tables IV and V we may see at a glance the color-preferences of any one poet, so far as these are indicated by the frequency with which he uses his different hues. Numerically judged, Whites usually have the preference, forming from one-fourth to one-third of the poet's total color-effects. In Milton they are nearly equaled by Greens and Blacks, and in Thomson by Reds. In Wordsworth's scale they are slightly subordinate to Greens. In Cowper's list alone do they fall to the third place. Purples and Browns divide the honor of standing lowest.

The average or normal poetic scale, as deduced from the totals of Table II, is White, Red, Black, Green, Yellow, Blue, Gray, Purple, Brown. If the average of the Romantic poets' color-scales be struck, it will differ from the above only by placing Blue above Yellow (Table V).

Of the poets, taken individually, Coleridge comes nearest to the normal scale. Scott elevates Gray and depresses Yellow; Wordsworth brings Green to the foremost place and considerably lowers Black; Byron puts Black above Red, and Blue above Green; Shelley so far neglects Red that it drops to the sixth place; Keats's chief eccentricity is the neglect of Black.

In general, those poets who concern themselves pronouncedly with depicting their fellow-men either in the drama, the tale, or the satire (Shakspere, Pope, Scott, Byron) secure 65 per cent. to 75 per cent. of their color-effects with Neutrals and Reds, while those who combine with the interest in Man a strong interest in a real or an imagined Nature (Milton, Thomson, Wordsworth, Shelley) choose for about 50 per cent. of their color-effects Greens, Blues, Purples, and Browns.

The right-hand column in Table II shows emphatically how greatly the use of color increased in English verse between the sixteenth century and the end of the eighteenth. The Romanticists show a uniformly high average. Even Wordsworth,

¹ Hues counted as indefinite are : pale, pallid, wan, dark, dusky, lurid, flush, blush, etc.

the least lavish among them, nearly doubles the color of Shakspere.

⟶ The theme, of course, determines in part the character and amount of color in a poem, narrative or descriptive verse being more lavishly colored than dramatic or didactic. ⟵Shakspere's low average is to some extent explained by the fact that the bulk of his work is dramatic, and the wealth of color-use by Scott and Keats is doubtless in part accounted for by the descriptive and narrative character of their verse. But one must not forget that much of the verse of Byron and Shelley is in dramatic form, nor that much of that of Coleridge and Wordsworth is speculative and philosophic; yet, in spite of these facts, each of these poets has a high color-average.

When all is said, we must concede to the Romanticists not only a full and much-differentiated vocabulary, as before proven, but a uniformly lavish and well-balanced use of that vocabulary.

III. POETIC COLOR-DISTRIBUTION.

In the third set of tables colors are classified according to their distribution in the fields which I have called A–Z (p. 113). The color-distribution of individual poets is first shown : Table VI gives their actual number of uses in each field ; Table VII reduces these to percentages. The accompanying Charts A and B list the various hues seen by the different poets in certain special fields of interest.

The figures of Table VII show at a glance the strongest color-interests of individual poets, and usually corroborate our judgment regarding their chosen fields of interest as revealed in their work as a whole. The most pronounced preferences shown here are in Shakspere's A 52 ; Thomson's G 21, H 27, I 10 ; Wordsworth's H 31; and Shelley's G 28 ; all of which harmonize perfectly with Shakspere's preference, as a dramatist, for the study of Man, with the new interest in the varied aspects of Nature shown by Thomson, with Wordsworth's love of fields and hills, and with Shelley's ardor for what Watson terms :

the pavilioned firmament o'erdoming all.
—*Shelley's Centenary.*

In this Table the poets before Milton show a pre-eminent interest in Man's form, his dress, and the works of his hands, as seen in the percentages quoted under A, B, and C respectively. They were familiar with the common aspects of Nature, but content to paint them without much variation of hue. It would seem that the external world appealed to them very little except as a background for human action, its artistic or æsthetic possibilities not entering into their thought. To Chaucer, for instance, fields and woods and leaves were invariably "green," as if they caught his eye only in the glad springtime. The distance attracted him but little, hues of mountain or horizon never receiving mention in his verse, and those of the sky and sea playing a very small part there. He was the poet of the near and the human. And such, in their different characters, were Langland and Gower, Spenser and Shakspere.

With Milton there is a new distribution of color. Only 32 per cent. falls under A, B, C, and Z,[1] as against Shakspere's 72 per cent.; while F, G, H, and I receive 60 per cent., as against Shakspere's 19 per cent.

In Thomson the Nature-interest is still more pronounced (67 per cent. to F, G, H, and I). He becomes the forerunner of the Romanticists. We may, indeed, go further and say that he even eclipsed them in the relative proportion of his Nature-coloring; for he leaves the field of human coloring almost untouched, while they show the double interest which links them on the one side with Shakspere, on the other with their prophet, Thomson. To the colors of dress and manufactures he pays the slightest possible heed, as may be seen by comparing his B and C with the same classes in other poets.

Cowper shows a pronounced interest in Man, but his individuality as a colorist is better exhibited in the more specific and smaller fields of Nature-study — not sky, plain, and sea, but animals and flowers. The two last-named classes, D and F, are relatively stronger in Cowper than in any other poet of our tables. In F are included fruits and specially-noted trees;

[1] Z may be counted in with the human color, since under it fall human qualities and abstractions.

when we have this fact in mind, Cowper's preference for D and F seems but natural in the owner of the pet hare, and the man whose memory could reconstruct from the naked shoots of mid-winter such a brilliant and fragrant garden as that described in *The Task*, VI, 140–80.

The strongest individual preferences of the Romanticists, as mentioned just above, exhibit fuller attention to all of the Nature-fields, and a less partial distribution of color, than do those of the representative poets of any earlier schools of English poetry. The results of further study of their color in its totality are tabulated in the two tables, VIII and IX.

We see first in VIII the Romantic distribution of each of the nine color-groups, and can determine at a glance the fields in which it has been most often applied. For example, 28 per cent. of the Reds is applied to the human body, 21 per cent. to the sky, and smaller proportional shares to the other fields of interest. Yellows go chiefly to atmospheric and celestial phe-nomena, being connected with the sun and its light. Thirty-nine per cent. of the Browns and the Grays are used on the human body, the second largest amount in each case going to earth and rocks. Class H naturally receives the lion's share of the Greens ; Class G takes 38 per cent. of the Blues and 29 per cent. of the Purples. Nearly half of the Blacks and the Whites goes to human skin and to sky. Taking Classes A–C together to represent human color-ing, we see that the colors most used by the portrait-painting poet are Reds, Browns, Whites, Grays, and Blacks ; while the land-scape painter dips his brush oftenest into Yellows, Greens, Blues, and Purples.

The figures of Table VIII were obtained by adding together the total color-usages of the six Romanticists, arranged accord-ing to the nine color-groups, and reducing the results to per-centages. From the same figures, arranged and added this time according to the twelve fields of interest, we obtain the percent-ages presented in Table IX. The only difference in the color-classification between this and other tables is that in this one *ten* color-groups have been included, the tenth being styled *Indefinites*, and having placed under it all such indefinite terms as "pale,"

" pallid," " wan," " lurid," " dark," " dusky," " flush," and " blanch."

In this Table IX we may note, first, that the Indefinites play their largest part in Class A, and, secondly, that Whites, Grays, and Blacks come next after Indefinites in this class, so that, all told, but 25 per cent. of the color used on Man is definite and bright. The color-scale for Class B (clothing) is White, Red, Black, Blue, Green, Purple, Yellow, Gray, Indefinites, Brown ; for Class G (the sky, etc.) it is Blue, Indefinites, equal parts of Red, Yellow, and White, Black, Gray; in H (vegetation) Green far outstrips other hues, being followed at a distance by Indefinites, Grays, and Blacks, and Whites, Reds, and Browns ; I (forms of water) shows a color-scale in which Whites and Blues lead, in about equal amounts, followed in order by Indefinites, Greens, Reds, Yellows, and Blacks, Purples, Browns, and Grays. For abstractions the commonest color by far is Black, 33 per cent.; among bright hues, however, Reds and Blues lead. These enumerations suggest others which may readily be drawn from the table itself.

If now we turn to Charts A and B, we shall find strikingly portrayed there the history of poetic color-vocabulary and color-distribution in their most salient phases. Here is a chronological presentation of the terms for color applied by poets, from the fourteenth to the nineteenth centuries, to Man's eyes, his hair, and his skin (Chart A); and to sky, vegetation, mountains, and deep waters (Chart B).

The first thing evident as one looks at A is the fact that there have been two great periods of definite interest in actual, concrete human coloring, and that these periods culminate as the sixteenth and eighteenth centuries pass into the seventeenth and nineteenth. Between the two the color-tide ebbs, with Goldsmith as an exponent of its lowest stage. The poetry of the seventeenth and eighteenth centuries departed from the real, interesting itself in the distant, the abstract, the philosophic. It described, not fellow-men, but the generalized species Man ; and in such description the coloring became, not unnaturally, meager and indefinite.

Let us now turn to Chart B. Here, in the Nature-hues, we

do not observe, as in A, two well-balanced periods, but a gradually increasing accentuation of color and a steady gain in nice
discriminations, until Langland's single hue "green" has grown
into the long, varied, nicely discriminated vocabularies of Scott,
Wordsworth, and Shelley. Thomson forms a little advance wave,
it is true, after whom the tide ebbs to Goldsmith again, but
Thomson's work is preparatory and premonitory of the Romanticists rather than representative of his own time. Construe
these lists in B as we may, they show that the color-study of
Nature's varied phases is a growth of modern times, scarcely
entered upon before the time of Thomson, and developed in
fullness—during the centuries covered in our tables—by the
Romanticists alone.

Now, when we put together Charts A and B, and bear in mind
the many points already noted as to the difference between the
Elizabethans and the Romanticists in the use of color, we may make
one or two still broader generalizations. While the Elizabethans,
as represented by Shakspere and Spenser, had an extensive vocabulary, their field of interest is, roughly speaking, limited to Man.
But the Romanticists, while retaining to the full this early interest in Man, added to it an equal or greater interest in Nature,
with an increase in discrimination in this field exactly parallel
to the increase in discrimination between Chaucer and Shakspere
in the earlier field. This dual interest, this subtle observation
of both Man and Nature, which characterizes the Romantic
School, is not a mere parallelization of two distinct threads of
sympathy, the one manifest in one poet or group of poems,
the second chosen and followed out by others ; it is an inextri-
cable interweaving, in each poet of the school, of the two strains
of thought. Man and Nature are conceived, even by Byron, as
connected, interdependent, and mutually influential ; and on
this closeness of relationship there depends that dignifying of
the senses which, with the greater pantheism from which it
springs, was first developed by Wordsworth, and has been continued on the same strong but delicate lines by Browning and
Tennyson. Color was to Wordsworth but one of the media
through which, as through all else sensuous, he perceived Eter-

nal Truth ; yet he treated it with the same fidelity and sincerity
which he devoted to the pursuit of his larger aim.   By the greater
of his successors, especially by Tennyson and Browning, color
has been handled with the same inevitable directness, the same
wide range of perception, the same delicate accuracy, the same
dignity of treatment, so marked in the Romanticists ; yet in
reviewing the use of color in English poetry, so far as it can be
analyzed and reported, one inevitably selects, as the most interesting phase of its rise to poetic importance, that moment in
which the equal value and interdependence of the two great
fields of sympathetic study were first fully recognized, the age of
Scott and Wordsworth, of Shelley and Keats.

I. COLOR-VOCABULARY.

Classified vocabularies of —   PAGE

    Langland, · · · · · · · · 103

    Gower, · · · · · · · · · · 104

    Chaucer, · · · 104

    Spenser, · · · · · · · · 104

    Shakspere, · · · · · · · 105

    Milton, · · · · · · · · 105

    Pope, · · · · · · · · · · 106

    Thomson, · · · · · · · · 106

    Goldsmith, · · · · · · · · 107

    Gray, · · · · · · · · 107

    Cowper, · · · 107

    Scott, · · · · · · · 108

    Coleridge, · · · · 108

    Wordsworth, · · · · · 109

    Byron, · · · · · 109

    Shelley, · · · 110

    Keats, · · · · · · · · 110

Comparative vocabularies of Elizabethans and Romanticists, 111

Table I: Summary of Variants, · · · · 114

LANGLAND : VOCABULARY.

REDS 8 — red 7, ruddy 1.
YELLOWS 2 — gilt 1, tawny 1.
BROWNS 0.
GREENS 6 — green 6.
BLUES 1 — blo 1.
PURPLES 0.
WHITES 11 — enblanched 1, hoar 4, pale 1, white 5.
GRAYS 3 — gray 3.
BLACKS 1 — black 1.

    TOTAL 32, distributed in classes as follows : A 6, B 5, C 8, D 1, E 6, F 0, G 0, H 2, I 0, K 0, X 2, Z 2.

GOWER : VOCABULARY.

REDS 17 — red 13, ruddy 4.
YELLOWS 1 — yellow 1.
BROWNS 0.
GREENS 34 — green 34.
BLUES 3 — blue 2, heaven-coloured 1.
PURPLES 1 — purple 1.
WHITES 48 — bleached 1, fade 7, hoar 7, pale 12, white 20, snow-white 1.
GRAYS 4 — gray 3, steel 1.
BLACKS 20 — black 19, coal-black 1.
TOTAL 128, distributed in classes as follows : A 53, B 7, C 3, D 11, E 6, F 3, G 7, H 24, I 1, K 1, X 4, Z 8.

CHAUCER : VOCABULARY.

REDS 102 — bay 3, brazil 1, grain 1, madder 1, red 79, fire-red 1, rose-red 1, scarlet-red 1, rosy 4, ruby 1, ruddy 4, sanguine 3, scarlet 2.
YELLOWS 35 — citron 1, fallow 2, gild 4, gold 10, latoun 1, saffron 1, sunny 2, weld 1, yellow 13.
BROWNS 9 — brown 9.
GREENS 76 — green 75, gaudy green 1.
BLUES 17 — azure 2, blo 1, blue 10, pers 2, wachet 1, woad 1.
PURPLES 2 — purple 2.
WHITES 161 — ashen 6, bleached 1, box 1, hoar 8, ivory 1, pale 43, pallid 1, silver 2, snowy 2, wan 6, white 86, paper-white 1, snow-white 3.
GRAYS 15 — gray 14, leaden 1.
BLACKS 63 — black 60, dun 2, sable 1.
TOTAL 480, distributed in classes as follows : A 158, B 57, C 46, D 50, E 16, F 39, G 34, H 40, I 6, K 4, X 21, Z 9.

SPENSER : VOCABULARY.

REDS 125 — Assyrian (?) 1, bloody 7, blush 17, carnation 1, castory 1, cherry 1, copper 1, crimson 3, damask 1, flame 1, red 26, blood-red 3, crimson red 1, fiery red 3, rosy red 10, sanguine red 1, scarlet red 1, vermeil red 1, rosy 12, ruby 3, ruddy 7, sanguine 2, scarlet 8, vermeil 13.
YELLOWS 129 — brazen 2, gilt 13, golden 96, ochre 1, saffron 1, tawny 3, yellow 13.
BROWNS 8 — brown 3, rusty-brown 1, rusty 2, sunburnt 1, tanned 1.
GREENS 79 — emerald 1, green 72, gaudy green 1, pallid green 1, verdant 4.
BLUES 28 — azure 8, blue 13, pallid blue 1, cerulean 1, sapphire 2, sky-colored 1, watchet 2.
PURPLES 42 — purple 42.

WHITES 243—alabaster 3, ashy 1, chalky 1, cream 1, hoary 28, ivory 14, lily 12, marble 2, pale 22, pallid 6, pearl 3, silver 53, snowy 34, wan 8, white 37, lily white 8, milk white 7, snow white 3.

GRAYS 21—blunket 1, gray 15, hoary gray 5.

BLACKS 73—black 50, coal-black 6, tomb black 1, darksome 2, dun 1, duskish 2, ebon 3, pitchy 1, sable 6, swart 1.

TOTAL 748, distributed in classes as follows: A 325, B 110, C 47, D 49, E 0, F 57, G 36, H 60, I 34, K 1, X 24, Z 5.

SHAKSPERE : VOCABULARY.

REDS 309—bay 3, bloody 2, blush 95, carnation 2, incaradine 1, cherry 4, copper 1, coral 3, crimson 24, damask 7, flame-colored 1, flushing 1, gilt [as with blood] 4, gules 2, Malmsey-[nose] 1, peach-colored 2, red 103, bloody-red 1, fiery red 2, over-red 1, ripe-red 1, wax-red 1, roan 4, rosy 15, cheek-roses 1, ruby 9, ruddy 1, sanguine 4, scarlet 12, vermilion 1.

YELLOWS 112—amber 2, auburn 2, Cain-colored 1, fallow 1, flaxen 1, French-crown color 1, gilded 16, golden 41, saffron 4, sallow 1, straw-colored 1, sunny 2, tawny 9, orange-tawny 2, yellow 28.

BROWNS 35—brown 24, chestnut 1, freestone-colored 1, hazel 1, russet 2, sanded 1, sunburnt 3, tanned 2.

GREENS 97—emerald 1, green 88, deep green 1, grass green 1, Kendel green 2, seawater green 1, verdure 3.

BLUES 40—azure 4, black and blue 4, blue 30, heaven-hued 1, welkin 1.

PURPLES 23—purple 23.

WHITES 439—alabaster 3, argentine 1, ashy 3, paly ashes 1, blanch 1, bleach 3, cream 1, fair 19, frosty 2, hoar 3, ivory 6, lily 8, linen 1, pale 152, ashy-pale 1, cold-pale 1, maid-pale 1, pallid 1, paper 2, silver 42, snowy 1, tallow 1, wan 5, whey 1, white 159, lily-white 3, milk-white 6, pale-white 1, silver-white 4, snow-white 6.

GRAYS 35—gray 31, grisly 4.

BLACKS 234—black 180, coal-black 8, hell-black 1, raven-black 1, collied 2, dark 4, dun 4, dusky 4, ebon 3, inky 2, jet 1, nighted 1, pitchy 5, raven 2, sable 9, sooty 1, swart 6.

TOTAL 1,324, distributed in classes as follows: A 675, B 80, C 69, D 66, E 12, F 85, G 105, H 48, I 25, K 7, X 30, Z 122.

MILTON : VOCABULARY.

REDS 28—blush 2, carbuncle 1, carnation 2, red 3, cloudy-red 1, fiery-red 1, rosy red 1, rosy 6, roseate 1, ruby 3, ruddy 2, sanguine 2, ensanguined 1, vermeil 1, envermeil 1.

YELLOWS 35—amber 4, gold 24, verdant gold 1, sallow 1, tawny 2, yellow 3

BROWNS 9—brinded 2, brown 5, imbrowned 1, russet 1.

GREENS 44—green 35, verdant 9.

BLUES 20 — azure 5, blue 8, sapphire 7.
PURPLES 16 — grain 3, purple 12, impurpled 1.
WHITES 45 — argent 1, blank 1, hoar 4, pale 17, pearl 1, silver 5, wan 4, white 12.
GRAYS 14 — gray 14.
BLACKS 45 — black 27, dark 3, dun 2, dusky 4, ebon 1, jet 1, sable 6, swart 1.
　　TOTAL 256, distributed in classes as follows : A 47, B 23, C 8, D 13, E 6, F 31, G 52, H 54, I 14, K 2, X 0, Z 6.

POPE : VOCABULARY.

REDS 46 — blush 24, crimson 1, red 13, rose 2, roseate 1, rubric 1, ruby 1, ruddier 1, scarlet 1, sorrel 1.
YELLOWS 26 — gilded 4, golden 15, sallow 1, yellow 6.
BROWNS 14 — adust 2, bronze 2, brown 5, embrown 2, nutbrown 1, russet 1, sunburnt 1.
GREENS 45 — green 35, sea-green 1, verdant 9.
BLUES 16 — azure 3, blue 10, black and blue 1, livid 2.
PURPLES 14 — purple 12, Tyrian 2.
WHITES 91 — argent 1, fair 1, hoary 4, ivory 1, milky 1, pale 20, pallid 1, silver 29, snowy 1, white 30, milk-white 2.
GRAYS 6 — grey 6.
BLACKS 39 — black 23, darksome 1, dun 1, dusky 1, jetty 1, sable 11, swarthy 1,
　　TOTAL 297, distributed in classes as follows : A 88, B 21, C 24, D 32, E 3, F 21, G 17, H 42, I 22, K 11, X 12, Z 4.

THOMSON : VOCABULARY.

REDS 85 — bay 1, blush 23, carnation 1, crimson 5, damask 1, flaming 2, flush 3, red 24, black-red 1, rosy 14, roseate 3, ruddy 4, sanguine 1, ensanguined 1, vermilion 1.
YELLOWS 41 — gilded 6, gold 6, lurid 2, sallow 1, sunny 1, tawny 2, tawny-orange 1, yellow 22.
BROWNS 34 — brazen 1, brindled 1, brown 17, dark brown 1, embrowned 6, fiery brown 1, iron brown 1, russet brown 1, iron 1, russet 3, sunburnt 1.
GREENS 76 — green 41, dark green 1, deep green 1, sea-green 1, wan-green 1, verdant 31.
BLUES 53 — azure 14, blue 25, cerulean 7, indigo 1, livid 6.
PURPLES 15 — purple 11, empurpled 1, white-empurpled 1, violet 2.
WHITES 90 — blank 1, bleaching 1, hoary 8, marble 1, pale 19, pallid 1, silver 8, snowy 7, wan 2, white 41, snowy white 1.
GRAYS 13 — gray 12, leaden 1.
BLACKS 75 — black 48, dark 3, sooty-dark 1, dun 8, dusky 5, ebon 1, jet 3, raven 1, sable 5.
　　TOTAL 482, distributed in classes as follows : A 74, B 6, C 10, D 26, E 8, F 43, G 99, H 132, I 49, K 5, X 14, Z 15.

GRAY : VOCABULARY.

REDS 18 — bloom 1, blush 7, crimson 1, red 1, rosy 5, ruddy 1, sanguine 1, vermeil 1.
YELLOWS 12 — amber 1. gilded 3, golden 7, tortoise 1.
BROWNS 2 — brown 2.
GREENS 11 — emerald 1, green 7, verdant 3.
BLUES 9 — azure 4, blue 4, sapphire 1.
PURPLES 5 — purple 4, violet 1.
WHITES 20 — faded 1, hoary 4, pale 3, pallid 2, silver 2, snowy 2, wan 3, white 3.
GRAYS 0.
BLACKS 12 — black 3, dusky 2, ebon 1, jet 1, sable 5.
TOTAL 89, distributed in classes as follows : A 26, B 6, C 4, D 7, E 0, F 6, G 13, H 13, I 4, K 1, X 0, Z 9.

GOLDSMITH : VOCABULARY.

REDS 6 — damask 1, red 1, rouge 1, ruddy 3.
YELLOWS 1 — yellow-blossomed 1.
BROWNS 3 — brown 2, nut-brown 1.
GREENS 3 — green 3.
BLUES 0.
PURPLES 1 — purple 1.
WHITES 4 — pale 1, white 3.
GRAYS 2 — gray 2.
BLACKS 6 — black 4, lamp-black 1, dusky 1.
TOTAL 26, distributed in classes as follows : A 6, B 7, C 6, D 0, E 0, F 1, G 1, H 4, I 0, K 0, X 1, Z 0.

COWPER : VOCABULARY.

REDS 65 — auburn 3, bloom 1, blush 22, crimson 3, mantling 2, orient 1, red 14, rosy 8, ruby 1, ruddy 2, sanguine 1, ensanguined 1, scarlet 6.
YELLOWS 30 — flaxen 1, gilded 7, golden 16, tawny 2, yellow 4.
BROWNS 9 — brown 4, russet 5.
GREENS 42 — green 33, dark-green 2, deep-green 1, gilded-green 1, verdant 5.
BLUES 18 — azure 5, black and blue 1, blue 9, cerulean 2, livid 1.
PURPLES 7 — purple 7.
WHITES 43 — blanch 1, bleaching 1, hoary 4, ivory 2, lily 1, pale 9, silver 6, snowy 6, wan 3, white 9, snowy white 1.
GRAYS 14 — badger-colored 1, gray 12, wannish gray 1.
BLACKS 25 — black 12, dark 3, ebon 2, sable 6, swarthy 2.
TOTAL 253, distributed in classes as follows : A 65, B 9, C 21, D 20, E 0, F 46, G 26, H 48, I 4, K 0, X 0, Z 14.

SCOTT : VOCABULARY.

REDS 301 — auburn 1, bay 1, bloody 4, blooming 1, blushing 44, crimson 25 flushed 9, gules 1, hectic 2, red 147, blood-red 10, dark red 8, fiery red 1, paly red 1, swarthy red 1, roan 1, red roan 1, rose 12, paly rose 1, ruby 1, ruddy 23, sanguine 1, scarlet 5.

YELLOWS 75 — amber 1, fallow 2, flaxen 5, gilded 15, gold 29, paly gold 1, lurid 2, or 1, saffron 1, sallow 1, sunny 1, tawny 4, yellow 12.

BROWNS 70 — brindled 1, brown 40, embrowned 3, berry-brown 1, dark-brown 6, deeper brown 1, nut-brown 2, ruddy-brown 1, chestnut 1, hazel 5, russet 5, sunburnt 4.

GREENS 142 — emerald 6, green 109, dark green 2, emerald green 1, fairy green 1, forest-green 1, hunter's green 1, Kendal green 1, light green 1 Lincoln green 7, sepulchral green 1, verdant 12.

BLUES 96 — azure 17, blue 68, dark blue 3, deadly blue 2, light blue 1, livid blue 2, pale blue 1, livid 2.

PURPLES 29 — purple-amethyst 1, purple 26, empurpled 2.

WHITES 348 — argent 2, ashen 2, blanch 4, bleach 4, fair 8, hoary 23, ivory 1, light 1, lily 2, pale 107, ashy pale 1, pallid 8, pearl 1, silver 63, snowy 22, wan 11, white 75, lily-white 2, milk-white 5, silver-white 3, snow-white 3.

GRAYS 156 — gray 153, pale gray 3.

BLACKS 277 — black 52, coal-black 4, jet-black 1, dark 95, dun 20, dusky 4, ebon 1, jet 6, raven 3, sable 64, swarthy 27.

TOTAL 1,494, distributed in classes as follows : A 474, B 116, C 158, D 101, E 18, F 70, G 204, H 239, I 92, K 7, X 7, Z 8.

COLERIDGE : VOCABULARY.

REDS 93 — auburn 2, bloody 2, blush 19, copper 1, crimson 6, fire 2, flush 4, pinky-silver 1, red 32, dark red 1, dun-red 1, rosy 15, roseate 1, ruby 1, scarlet 5.

YELLOWS 24 — amber 3, golden 10, lurid 2, yellow 9.

BROWNS 5 — brown 3, dark brown 1, russet 1.

GREENS 74 — emerald 1, green 6, dark green 2, yellow-green 1, verdant 4.

BLUES 48 — azure 2, blue 41, skiey blue 1, cerulean 1, livid 2, sapphire 1.

PURPLES 19 — amethyst 1, purple 17, impurpled 1.

WHITES 160 — fair 1, hoary 8, lily 2, milky 1, pale 54, pallid 4, silver 11, snowy 7, wan 16, white 51, maiden-white 1, milk-white 1, snow-white 3.

GRAYS 16 — grey 16.

BLACKS 82 — black 53, blue-black 1, coal-black 2, jet-black 1, dark 11, dusky 1, ebon 2, pitchy 1, raven 2, sable 7, swart 1.

TOTAL 521, distributed in classes as follows : A 166, B 23, C 16, D 25, E 9, F 67, G 91, H 72, I 23, K 2, X 1, Z 26.

WORDSWORTH : VOCABULARY.

REDS 129 — bloom 6, blush 11, carnation 1, crimson 15, fiery 2, flame 2, flush 3, pink 1, red 33, blood-red 1, deep-red 1, dull-red 4, military-red 2, rosy-red 1, rosy 19, roseate 4, ruby 1, ruddy 9, scarlet 10, martial scarlet 1, vermilion 2.

YELLOWS 110 — amber 2, fallow 1, gilded 10, golden 58, lurid 3, orange 2, saffron 1, sallow 1, tawny 4, deep yellow 1, yellow 27.

BROWNS 29 — bronzed 1, brown 12, embrown 1, dark brown 2, Egyptian brown 1, iron-brown 1, red-brown 1, hazel 1, russet 1, rusty 2, sunburnt 6.

GREENS 295 — emerald 4, green 269, gloomy green 1, grass-green 1, leaf-green 1, olive green 1, pea-green 1, sea green 1, tawny green 1, verdant 15.

BLUES 124 — azure 22, blue 80, black-blue 1, dark blue 2, gloomy blue 1, pale blue 1, sable blue 1, sapphire blue 1, sky-blue 2, cerulean 10, harebell 1, sapphire 2.

PURPLES 39 — grain-tinctured 1, purple 30, purpureal 4, empurpled 2, Tyrian 1, violet 1.

WHITES 286 — alabaster 1, blanch 1, bleach 3, ghastly 1, hoary 35, marble 1, pale 49, pallid 14, silver 46, wan 11, white 98, milk-white 7, pearly-white 2, snow-white 17.

GRAYS 92 — grey 91, silver-grey 1.

BLACKS 111 — black 63, coal-black 1, dark 31, dusky 6, ebon 2, jet 1, raven 1, sable 4, sooty 1, Stygian 1.

TOTAL 1,215, distributed in classes as follows : A 217, B 57, C 50, D 81, E 9, F 123, G 208, H 379, 1 70, K 2, X 4, Z 15.

BYRON : VOCABULARY.

REDS 282 — auburn 8, bloom 7, blush 70, swarthy black 1, carnation 2, incarnadine 2, copper 1, coral 1, crimson 28, flame 1, flushed 10, hectic 3, pink 1, pomegranate 1, red 89, autumnal-leaf-like red 1, blood-red 7, dark red 1, dusky red 1, gory red 1, roan 1, rose 26, rouged 1, ruby 1, ruddy 2, sanguine 2, scarlet 9, vermilion 3.

YELLOWS 102 — amber 2, buff 1, flaxen 1, flesh-colored 1, gild 25, gold 25, lurid 1, orange 2, saffron 4, sallow 7, sulphurous 1, yellow 32.

BROWNS 22 — brazen 1, bronze 2, ruddy bronze 1, brown 6, dark-brown 1, light-brown 1, nut-brown 2, brunette 1, chestnut 1, hazel 1, mahogany 1, sunburnt 4.

GREENS 110 — emerald 7, green 82, dark-green 3, deep green 1, dull green 1, dusky green 1, sea green 1, verdant 14.

BLUES 193 — azure 23, alpine azure 1, blue 139, dark-blue 11, deep-blue 8, pale-blue 2, cerulean 1, livid 7, sapphire 1.5

PURPLES 48 — hyacinthine 1, lilac 1, purple 40, empurpled 2, deep-purple 2, purple hectic 1, violet 1.

WHITES 360 — ashes 2, blanch 1, bleach 2, blonde 1, fair 22, hoar 38, ivory 1, marble 1, pale 108, pallid 6, pearl 2, silver 17, snowy 15, swanlike 1, wan 4, waxen 1, white 133, milk-white 3, snow-white 2.

GRAYS 58 — gray 56, dark-gray 1, silver-gray 1.

BLACKS 330 — black 158, coal-black 2, death-black 1, jet-black 2, dark 75, dun 12, dusky 18, ebon 1, inky 1, jet 4, raven 9, sable 35, sooty 1, swarthy 11.

TOTAL 1,515, distributed in classes as follows : A 639, B 122, C 131, D 35, F 15, F 35, G 135, H 149, I 131, K 9, X 22, Z 92.

SHELLEY : VOCABULARY.

REDS 142 — blush 7, death-blushing 1, crimson 21, faint-crimson 1, dawn-tinted 1, flush 9, gore 1, gules 1, pink 1, red 66, blood-red 7, dark-red 2, rosy 8, roseate 3, ruddy 3, sanguine 5, rose-ensanguined 1, vermilion 4.

YELLOWS 158 — amber 2, brimstone 1, gilded 1, golden 109, purple gold 1, deep-red gold 1, heaven-colored 1, lurid 8, orange 4, sallow 1, sulphurous 4, waxen 2, yellow 23.

BROWNS 14 — bacon 1, brinded 1, brown 11, iron 1.

GREENS 183 — chrysolite 3, emerald 15, glaucous 1, green 153, dark green 5, deep green 1, sea green 2, verdant 3.

BLUES 182 — azure 66, blue 96, dark blue 6, lurid blue 1, pale blue 2, livid 3, sapphire 8.

PURPLES 52 — amethyst 5, purple 42, purpureal 1, dark purple 1, deepest purple 1, pale purple 1, violet 1.

WHITES 514 — alabaster 1, argentine 1, ashy 1, blanch 2, bleach 1, fair 4, hoary 53, ivory 1, marble 4, milky 1, moonlight colored 2, pale 196, pallid 20, pearl 3, silver 45, snowy 15, wan 34, white 123, milk-white 4, snow-white 2, wool-white 1.

GRAYS 99 — ashen 1, cinereous 1, grey 92, dark grey 1, hoary grey 1, leaden-colored 3.

BLACKS 160 — black 74, hell-black 1, night-black 1, dark 60, darksome 2, dun 9, dusky 3, ebon 4, inky 1, pitchy 1, swart 4.

TOTAL 1,504, distributed in classes as follows: A 380, B 24, C 77, D 51, E 16, F 111, G 419, H 214, I 127, K 6, X 10, Z 69.

KEATS : VOCABULARY.

REDS 121 — auberne 1, bloom 4, blush 22, cherry 1, coral 1, crimson 8, damask 3, flush 12, gules 1, pink 3, red 16, blood-red 3, rosy 17, roseate 1, ruby 4, rubious 1, rubious-argent 1, ruddy 6, sanguineous 1, scarlet 6, vermilion 9.

YELLOWS 123 — amber 8, ardent 1, fallow 1, gild 2, golden 100, sober gold 1, tawny 2, yellow 7, volcanian yellow 1.

BROWNS 14 — bronzed 3, brown 7, hazel 1, olive 1, sunburnt 1, tann'd 1.

GREENS 123 — emerald 5, green 99, beechen-green 1, blue-green 1, dark green
1, deep green 1, forest-green 1, gold green 1, grass green 1, light green 2,
Lincoln green 1, meadow green 1, verdant 9.

BLUES 76 — azure 6, black and blue 1, blue 52, dark blue 4, deep blue 1, light
blue 2, cerulean 1, livid 1, sapphire 7, turquoise 1.

PURPLES 30 — amethyst 4, purple 24, empurple 1, dark violet 1.

WHITES 310 — alabaster 1, argent 5, blanched 3, creamy 2, fair 2, ivory 5, lily
8, marble 2, milky 4, pale 55, death-pale 2, pallid 6, pearly 5, silver 78, wan
silver 1, snowy 8, starlight 1, wan 9, white 95, frost-white 1, lily-white 2,
milk-white 4, silver-white 1, snow-white 1.

GRAYS 25 — grey 24, dark grey 1.

BLACKS 79 — black 29, jet-black 1, dark 19, dun 3, dusky 3, ebon 7, jet 5, raven
2, sable 2, sooty 1, swart 7.

TOTAL 901, distributed in classes as follows : A 243, B 43, C 80, D 77 E
16, F 96, G 150, H 103, I 37, K 12, X 13, Z 31.

COMPARATIVE VOCABULARY.

The color-vocabulary of the *sixteenth century*, as represented by Spenser
and Shakspere, and that of the *Romantic Period*, as represented by Scott, Coleridge, Wordsworth, Byron, Shelley, and Keats.

Words found only in the Elizabethan vocabulary are placed between
brackets [ ]; those found only in the Romantic, between parentheses ( ).
Words common to the two stand without either.

REDS : [Assyrian], (auburn), bay, bloody, (bloom), blush, (death-blushing)
(swarthy-blush), carnation, incarnadine, [castory], cherry, copper, coral,
crimson, damask, (dawn-tinted), (fiery), flame-coloured, flush, [gilt (as with
blood)], gore, gules, (hectic), (purple-hectic), [Malmsey], [peach-coloured],
(pink), (pinky-silver), (pomegranate), red, (autumnal-leaf-like-red), blood-
red, [crimson-red], (dark-red), (deep-red), (dull-red), (dun-red), (dusky-
red), fiery-red, (gory-red), (military-red), (paly-red), rose-red, [sanguine-
red], [scarlet-red], (swarthy-red), [vermeil-red], [wax-red], roan, (red-
roan), rosy, [cheek-roses], (paly-rose), (roseate), (rouged), ruby, (rubious),
(rubious-argent), ruddy, sanguine, (sanguineous), (rose-ensanguined), scarlet, vermeil or vermilion.

YELLOWS : amber, (ardent), [auberne], (brimstone), (buff), [Cain-coloured],
fallow, flaxen, (flesh-coloured), [French-crown-coloured], gilded, golden,
(deep-red-gold), (paly-gold), (purple-gold), (sober-gold), (heaven-coloured),
(lurid), [ochre], (or), (orange), saffron, sallow, [straw-coloured], sunny,
(sulphurous), tawny, [orange-tawny], (topaz), (waxen), yellow, (deep vol-
canian-yellow).

BROWNS : (bacon), (brazen), (bronzed), (brinded), brown, (embrowned), (berry-
brown), (dark-brown), (deep-brown), (Egyptian-brown), (iron-brown),
(light-brown), (nut-brown), (red-brown), (ruddy-brown), [rusty-brown],

(brunette), chestnut, [freestone-coloured], hazel, (iron), (mahogany), (olive), russet, rusty, [sanded], sunburnt, tanned.

GREENS: (chrysolite), emerald, (glaucous), green, (beechen-green), (blue-green), (dark-green), deep-green, (dull-green), (dusky-green), (emerald-green), (evergreen), (forest-green), [gaudy-green], (gloomy-green), (gold-green), grass-green, (hunter's green), Kendal-green, (leaf-green), (light-green), (Lincoln-green), (meadow-green), (olive-green), [pallid-green], (pea-green), (sea-green), [sea-water-green], (sepulchral-green), (tawny-green), (yellow-green), verdant.

BLUES: azure, black-and-blue, blue, (black-blue), (dark-blue), (dead-blue), (deep-blue), (gloomy-blue), (light-blue), (livid-blue), (lurid-blue), (pale-blue), [pallid-blue], (sable-blue), (sapphire-blue), (skiey-blue), cerulean, (harebell), [heaven-hued], (livid), sapphire, [watchet], [sky-coloured], [welkin], (turquoise).

PURPLES: (amethyst), (purple-amethyst), (grain-tinctured), (hyacinthine), (lilac), purple, (purpureal), (dark-purple), (deepest-purple), (empurpled), (white-empurpled), (Tyrian), (violet), (dark-violet).

WHITES: alabaster, argent, ashen, blanch, bleach, (blonde), [chalky], cream, fair, [frosty], ghastly-hued, hoary, ivory, (light), lily, [linen-(faced)], marble, (milky), (moonlight-coloured), pale, ashy-pale, pale, [cold-pale], (death-pale), [maid-pale], pallid, [paper-(faced)], pearl, silver, (silver-wan), snowy, (starlight), (swanlike), [tallow-(faced)], wan, waxen, [whey-(faced)], white, (frost-white), lily-white, milk-white, [pale-white], (pearly-white), silver-white, snow-white, (wool-white).

GRAYS: [blunket], (cinereous), gray, (dark-gray), hoary-gray, (pale-gray), (silver-gray), [grizly-(hued)], (leaden-coloured).

BLACKS: black, (blue-black), coal-black, (death-black), hell-black, (jet-black), (night-black), [raven-black], [tomb-black], [collied], dark, dun, dusky, ebon, inky, jet, [nighted], pitchy, raven, sable, sooty, (Stygian), swart or swarthy.

NOTE.—I have uniformly used the hyphen in the compound hues listed above, although it is not always found in the texts from which I have catalogued.

II. COLOR-SCALE.

TABLE II: The actual number of each poet's uses of color, arranged under the nine color-groups, together with the total number of lines catalogued for each and the color average of each per 1,000 lines.

TABLE III: The percentage of color falling in each color-group, based on the figures of II. Also a division by percentages of each poet's total color in definite and indefinite hues.

TABLE IV: The ten color-words oftenest used by each poet, arranged in order of preference.

Table V. The nine color-groups arranged in order of frequency of use and thus showing each poet's color-scale.

III. COLOR-DISTRIBUTION.

SCHEME OF CLASSIFICATION.

I. MAN AND HIS WORKS.

A. *The Human Body:* skin, veins, blood, eyes, hair, nails, blemishes. Here are also included *gods, angels, demons, fairies, ghosts, mythological beings,* distinct *personifications,* and representations of any of these beings in art.

B. *The Attire* of man and of the other beings included under A, including feathers and furs when worn, war-gear, badges, and all adornments other than gems and flowers.

C. *Manufactured Articles:* weapons, implements, prepared food and drink, furniture, walls, buildings; also dens, caves, bowers, and the like, when spoken of as dwellings.

II. NATURE.

D. *Animal-life:* beasts, birds, fishes, insects; also natural animal products, such as honey, eggs, milk; not including shells and ivory.

E. *Minerals* (when not treated on a large scale): metals, gems, sands, ivory, marble, porphyry, and the like; shells, ashes.

F. *Flowers* and *Fruits,* with mosses and plants or trees mentioned by name, or selected for special notice.

G. *The Heavens* and their phenomena: clouds, air, mist, and atmospheric effects in general; heavenly bodies, smoke, flame.

H. *The Land* in its general aspects: fields, mountains, cliffs, woods, deserts, abysses, shadows; also ruins when part of landscape.

I. *The Waters:* ocean, lake, river, foam, dew, rain, frost, ice, snow.

K. *Miscellaneous objects: e. g.,* "things," "distant speck."

III. COLOR AS MERE COLOR.

X. *Hues,* pigments, dyestuffs.

IV. ABSTRACTIONS.

Z. Abstract qualities, or objects treated in a purely metaphorical or symbolical way, *e. g.,* "grene conscience," "red fury," "black heart."

Table VI: The actual number of each poet's color-uses arranged according to the twelve fields of interest noted in the scheme of classification.

Table VII: The percentage of color falling in each field of interest, based on the figures of VI.

Table VIII: Percentages, for the Romanticists as a body, showing how each color-group is distributed through the fields A–Z.

TABLE IX : Percentages, for the Romanticists as a body, showing for each field of interest the distribution of colors within it.

CHART A : Terms applied by all the poets catalogued to EYES, to HAIR, to SKIN.

CHART B : Terms applied by all the poets catalogued to SKY AND CLOUD, to VEGETATION, to MOUNTAINS, and to DEEP WATERS.

TABLE I.

Showing the number of variants used in each color-group.

	Reds	Yellows	Browns	Greens	Blues	Purples	Whites	Grays	Blacks	Total
Langland	2	2	..	1	1	..	4	1	1	12
Gower	2	1	..	1	2	1	6	2	2	17
Chaucer	13	9	1	2	6	1	13	2	3	50
Spenser	25	8	5	5	7	1	18	3	10	82
Shakspere	30	15	8	7	5	1	30	2	16	114
Milton	12	6	3	2	3	2	8	1	8	46
Pope	9	4	6	3	4	2	11	1	7	47
Thomson	13	8	10	6	5	3	11	2	9	67
Gray	8	4	1	3	3	2	8	..	5	34
Goldsmith	4	1	2	1	..	1	2	1	3	15
Cowper	13	5	2	5	5	1	11	3	5	49
Scott	23	13	11	12	8	2	21	2	11	103
Coleridge	14	4	3	5	6	2	13	1	11	59
Wordsworth	20	11	10	10	12	4	14	2	10	93
Byron	29	12	12	8	9	5	19	3	14	111
Shelley	17	13	4	8	7	6	21	4	10	90
Keats	19	9	6	13	10	3	25	2	11	96

TABLE II.

Showing for individual poets the number of times each color-group is used, the total number of lines counted, and the color-average per 1,000 lines.

	Reds	Yellows	Browns	Greens	Blues	Purples	Whites	Grays	Blacks	Totals	Number of lines catalogued	Color-words per 1,000 lines
Chaucer	102	35	9	76	17	2	161	15	63	480	34,109	14
Spenser	125	129	8	79	28	42	243	21	73	748	45.553	17
Shakspere ..	309	112	35	97	40	23	439	35	234	1324	106,204¹	12
Milton	28	35	9	44	20	16	45	14	45	256	16,987	15
Pope	46	26	14	45	16	14	91	6	39	297	10,287	29
Thomson ...	85	41	34	76	53	15	90	13	75	482	13,158	35
Cowper.....	65	30	9	42	18	7	42	14	25	252	20,145	12
Scott	303	75	70	143	96	29	348	156	297	1495	30,947	48
Coleridge ...	93	24	5	94	48	19	160	16	82	523	20,189	25
Wordsworth.	129	110	29	295	124	39	286	92	111	1215	55,343	22
Byron	282	105	22	111	196	47	361	58	329	1511	59,999	25
Shelley	142	158	14	183	182	52	515	98	160	1432	30,030	48
Keats.......	121	123	14	123	76	30	310	23	79	901	13,991	65

¹ Leopold edition.

TABLE III.

Showing the percentage of each color-group, for the poets named ; and in addition showing the percentages of definite and indefinite hues in each.

	Reds	Yellows	Browns	Greens	Blues	Purples	Whites	Grays	Blacks	Totals	Indefinites	Definites
Chaucer	21	7	2	16	4	1	33	3	13	100%	14	86
Spenser	17	17	1	11	3	5	34	3	10	100	10	90
Shakspere.......	24	9	3	7	3	2	33	3	16	100	24	76
Milton	11	14	3	17	8	6	18	6	17	100	16	84
Pope	15	9	5	15	6	5	30	2	13	100	20	30
Thomson........	18	8	7	16	11	3	18	3	16	100	17	83
Cowper.........	26	12	3	17	7	3	16	6	10	100	19	81
Scott	20	5+	5	9	6+	2	23	12	18	100	24	76
Coleridge	18	5	1	14	9	3	31	3	16	100	21	79
Wordsworth	10	9	3	24	10	4	23	8	9	100	15	85
Byron	19	7	1	7	13	3	24	4	22	100	25	75
Shelley	10	10	1	12	12	4	34	6	11	100	28	72
Keats..........	14	14	1	14	8	3	34	3	9	100	17	83

TABLE IV.

Chaucer		Spenser		Shakspere		Milton		Pope		Thomson		Cowper		Scott		Coleridge		Wordsworth		Byron		Shelley		Keats	
white	90	golden	96	black	100	green	35	green	35	black	48	green	37	red	169	green	69	green	276	black	164	pale	196	green	109
red	82	green	74	white	179	black	27	white	32	green	45	blush	22	gray	156	black	57	white	134	blue	160	green	162	white	104
green	76	black	57	pale	155	gold	25	silver	30	white	41	gold	16	green	124	white	56	gray	92	white	139	white	130	golden	101
black	60	white	53	blush	109	pale	17	blush	24	verdant	30	red	14	pale	109	pale	54	blue	89	pale	109	golden	115	silver	79
pale	43	silver	53	red	95	black	13	black	22	brown	26	black	13	dark	95	blue	43	black	64	blue	90	blue	105	blue	59
gray	14	red	42	green	93	purple	13	pale	20	red	25	white	12	white	88	red	34	golden	58	green	90	gray	94	pale	57
yellow	13	purple	42	silver	42	white	8	golden	15	blue	24	blue	10	blue	77	blush	19	pale	49	dark	74	black	76	black	30
gold	10	snowy	33	golden	41	blue	8	purple	12	yellow	22	sable	9	sable	64	purple	18	silver	46	blush	71	red	75	purple	25
blue	10	hoary	28	gray	31	sapphire	7	red	12	blush	22	pale	9	silver	63	rosy	16	red	42	gray	58	azure	66	gray	25
brown	9	pale	22	blue	30	brown	6	blue	10	pale	18	rosy	8	brown	54	wan	16	purple	36	purple	44	dark	60	red	19
						red	6	verdant	9																	

TABLE V.

Chaucer		Spenser		Shakspere		Milton		Pope		Thomson		Cowper		Scott		Coleridge		Wordsworth		Byron		Shelley		Keats		Romantic average
Whites	161	Whites	243	Whites	439	Whites	45	Whites	91	Whites	90	Reds	66	Whites	348	Whites	160	Greens	295	Whites	361	Whites	515	Whites	310	Whites
Reds	102	Yellows	129	Reds	399	Blacks	45	Reds	46	Reds	85	Greens	43	Reds	301	Reds	93	Whites	286	Blacks	309	Greens	183	Greens	123	Reds
Greens	76	Reds	125	Blacks	234	Greens	44	Greens	45	Greens	75	Whites	41	Blacks	277	Blacks	82	Reds	129	Reds	284	Blues	182	Yellows	123	Blacks
Blacks	63	Greens	79	Yellows	112	Yellows	35	Blacks	39	Blacks	75	Yellows	30	Grays	142	Greens	74	Blues	124	Blues	195	Blacks	160	Reds	131	Greens
Yellows	35	Blacks	73	Greens	97	Reds	20	Yellows	26	Blues	53	Blacks	25	Greens	142	Blues	48	Blacks	111	Greens	110	Yellows	158	Blacks	76	Blues
Blues	17	Purples	42	Blues	40	Blues	14	Blues	16	Yellows	41	Blues	18	Blues	96	Yellows	24	Yellows	110	Yellows	105	Reds	142	Blues	76	Yellows
Grays	15	Blues	40	Browns	28	Purples	16	Purples	14	Browns	34	Grays	14	Yellows	75	Purples	19	Grays	92	Grays	58	Grays	98	Purples	30	Grays
Browns	9	Grays	35	Grays	35	Grays	14	Grays	6	Purples	15	Browns	9	Browns	70	Grays	16	Purples	39	Purples	47	Purples	52	Grays	25	Purples
Purples	2	Browns	8	Purples	23	Browns	9			Grays	13	Purples	7	Purples	29	Browns	5	Browns	39	Browns	22	Browns	14	Browns	14	Browns

TABLE VI.

Showing the *total number* of *words* in each *class.*

(Basis of Table VII.)

	A	B	C	D	E	F	G	H	I	K	X	Z	Totals
Chaucer.....	158	57	46	50	16	39	34	40	6	4	21	9	480
Spenser.....	325	110	47	49		57	36	60	34	1	24	5	948
Shakspere ...	675	80	69	65	12	85	105	48	26	7	30	122	1324
Milton	47	23	8	13	6	31	52	54	14	2		6	256
Pope	88	21	24	32	3	21	17	42	22	12	12	4	297
Thomson....	74	6	10	26	8	43	99	130	49	5	14	15	481
Cowper	65	10	20	20		46	26	47	4			14	252
Scott	474	116	158	101	18	70	204	239	92	7	7	8	1494
Coleridge ...	166	23	16	25	9	67	91	72	23	2	1	26	521
Wordsworth..	217	57	50	81	9	123	208	379	70	2	4	15	1215
Byron.......	639	122	131	35	15	35	135	149	131	9	22	92	1515
Shelley......	380	24	77	51	16	111	419	214	127	6	10	69	1504
Keats.......	243	43	80	77	16	96	150	103	37	12	13	31	901

TABLE VII.

Percentage of color falling in each *class.*

	A	B	C	D	E	F	G	H	I	K	X	Z	Totals
Chaucer	33	12	9	10	4	8	7	8	1	1	5	2	100%
Spenser...............	43	15	6	6		7	5	8	5	$\frac{1}{4}$	4	$\frac{3}{4}$	100
Shakspere	52	6	5	5	1	6	8	3	2	1	2	9	100
Milton...............	18	9	3	5	2	13	20	21	6	1		2	100
Pope.................	28	7	8	11	1	7	6	14	8	4	4	2	100
Thomson	16	1	2	5	2	9	21	27	10	1	3	3	100
Cowper........	26	4	8	8		18	10	18	2			6	100
Scott.................	32	8	10	7	1	5	13½	16	6	$\frac{1}{2}$	$\frac{1}{2}$	$\frac{1}{2}$	100
Coleridge	32	4	3	5	2	13	17	14	4	$\frac{7}{10}$	$\frac{7}{10}$	5	100
Wordsworth...........	17	5	4	7	1	10	17	31	6	$\frac{7}{10}$	$\frac{7}{10}$	1	100
Byron.........	42	8	9	2	1	2	9	10	8	1	2	6	100
Shelley	25	2	5	3	1	7	28	14	8	1	1	5	100
Keats	27	5	9	8	2	11	17	11	4	1	1	3	100

TABLE VIII.[1]

	A	B	C	D	E	F	G	H	l	K	X	Z	Totals
Reds	28	8	15	4	1	10	21	5	3	1	1	3	100%
Yellows	15	4	11	8	3	13	31	7	4	1	1	2	100
Browns	39	3	8	6		7	3	32	1		1		100
Greens	1	4	1	3	½	10	2	72	5	½	½	1	100
Blues	17	6	4	2	2	3	38	5	19		1	3	100
Purples	9	12	5	2	1	19	29	12	7		1	.5	100
Whites	27	8	10	11	1	6	16	5	13	½	1	1½	100
Grays	39	4	12	5	1	2	15	16	1		1	4	100
Blacks	27	9	10	7	1	3	12	12	4	1	2	12	100

TABLE IX.

	Reds	Yellows	Browns	Greens	Blues	Purples	Whites	Grays	Blacks	Indefinites	Totals
A	11	4	3	½	6	½	12	8	9	46	100%
B	18	.6	1	11	12	7	21	5	16	3	100
C	24	11	3	3	5	2	21	.11	13	7	100
D	10	11	2	7	4	1	32	6	15	12	100
E	17	23		4	17	6	16	4	10	7	100
F	16	14	2	18	4	8	13	2	4	19	100
G	14	14	1	1	22	5	14	5	7	17	100
H	4	3	4	56	3	2	4	7	7	10	100
I.	6	5	2	10	27	3	28	1	5	13	100
K	20	18		9			18	3	29	12	100
X	21	9	2	7	11	3	18	5	17	7	100
Z	12	4		6	11	3	7	7	33	17	100

[1] Tables VIII and IX sum up the figures of the six Romanticists.

CHART "A." COLOR-WORDS APPLIED TO MAN.

	LANGLAND	GOWER	CHAUCER	SPENSER	SHAKSPERE	MILTON	POPE	THOMSON
Terms for Eyes		gray heaven-colored	citryn gray red "betwixe yelw and reed"	sapphire (used as a noun)	black blue dark green gray hazel pale- pink pitch-red welkin		blue pale	azure blue pale
Terms for Hair	hoar	hoar white yellow	black gilt gold gray hoar red saffron sunny white yellow	black copper-colored golden gray hoary gray hoary silver white snow-white yellow	amber auburn black coal-black brown Cain-colored chestnut flaxen French-crown- frosty golden gray grizly hoar inky orange-tawhy purple-in-grain raven sable silver straw-colored sunny white silver-white yellow	golden gray white	gray red sable	black brown ebon gray hoary jet silver sunny white yellow
Terms for Skin	pale ruddy	bleche fade pale red ruddy white	ashen black blue box- brown fallow green ivory leaden pale pallid purple red fire-red rosy ruby ruddy sanguine scarlet snowy wan white	alabaster ashy black blue blush carnation cream crimson flame ivory lily marble pale pallid purple red rosy-red rosy ruddy silver snowy sunburnt swarthy tann'd tawny vermilion wan white lily-white milk-white	alabaster ashy azure black black & blue blanch blue blush brown cherry copper cream crimson damask dark dun fair flushing freestone green ivory lily linen- malmsey- pale paly ashes ashy pale cold pale maid pale pallid paper- raven red rosy ruby sable saffron tallow- sanguine sunburnt swart sooty wan whey-white lily-white milk-white pale-white snow-white yellow	blush dusky grain pale red rosy red swart vermeil wan white	adust black blue bronze brown nut-brown fair ivory livid pale pallid red rose sable sallow snowy sunburnt swarthy white	black blush brown carnation crimson jet livid pale red rosy roseate ruddy sable snowy vermilion white yellow

CHART "A," COLOR-WORDS APPLIED TO MAN.

GRAY	GOLDSMITH	COWPER	SCOTT	COLERIDGE	WORDSWORTH	BYRON	SHELLEY	KEATS
blue			azure black blue deadly blue light blue pale blue dark gray hazel lurid sable swarthy tawny	black blue dark red	azure black cerulean dark gray harebell sable	azure black blue deep blue dark gray dark gray red white	azure black blue dark blue brown dark green lurid pale red	blue deep blue dark deep green pale violet
hoary		auburn flaxen golden gray hoary silver white	amber auburn black coal-black jet-black bleached brown dark-brown nut-brown dark fair golden paly gold gray hazel hoary jet light raven red sable silver snowy white silver-white yellow	auburn jet-black green gray hoary sable silver white yellow	black coal-black brown dark-brown dark dusky golden gray silver-gray hoary red rusty silver white snow-white yellow	auburn black brown dark-brown light-brown chestnut dark fair flaxen golden gray silver-gray green hazel hoar hyacinthine inky jet raven red sable silver white yellow	black brown fair golden gray hoary gray green hoary silver white snow-white yellow	auburn black ebon golden gray hoar jet white frost-white snow-white
bloom blush dusky faded pale pallid purple rosy sable wan white	brown damask dusky pale red ruddy	black black & blue blue bloom blushing lily mantling orient pale red rosy sable snowy swarthy tawny wan white	ashen black blanch blooming blue blush brown ruddy-brown crimson dark fair flush golden hectic ivory lily livid pale ashy pale pallid red blood-red dark-red rosy paly rose ruddy sable snowy sunburnt swarthy wan white	black blue blush brown crimson dark flush lily livid lurid pale pallid purple red rosy roseate sable scarlet snowy swart wan white	black blanch blush brown Egyptian brown carnation dark dusky flushed marble pale pallid empurpled red deep red roseate rosy ruddy wan white snow white yellow	ashes black blanched blonde blush swarthy blush bronze nut-brown brunette carnation copper coral crimson dark dusky fair flame flushed hectic ivory livid mahogany marble pallid pale pomegranate purple red autumnal-leaf-like-red blood-red rosy rouge ruddy sable sallow snowy sooty sunburnt swan-like swarthy wan white yellow	alabaster ashen black blanched blue blushing brimstone brown crimson fair flushed green marble milky pale pallid red rosy ruddy sallow snowy swart vermilion wan waxen white yellow	azure black black & blue blanch bloomed blush bronzed brown creamy damask dark dusky flushed ivory lily marble milky olive pale pallid pearly red rosy sanguineous silver snowy starlight swart wan white lily-white

CHART "B," COLOR-WORDS APPLIED TO NATURE.

	LANGLAND	GOWER	CHAUCER	SPENSER	SHAKSPERE	MILTON	POPE	THOMSON
Terms for SKY, CLOUD, AIR		black	black, blue, gray, rosy	azure, black, coal-black, brazen, crimson, darksome, golden, purple, ruddy	azure, black, blue, blush, golden, gray, pale, purple, red, fiery-red, russet, silver, white	amber, azure, black, blue, blushing, dun, dusky, ebon, golden, gray, red, sable, silver, white	argent, blush, gilded, golden, purple	azure, blue, black, brazen, cerulean, crimson, dun, dusky, golden, gray, leaden, livid, pale, pallid, red, black-red, rosy, roseate, white, yellow
Terms for VEGETATION (not including flowers, fruits, and mosses)	green	green	green	green, pallid green, pallid	emerald, green, grass-green, gold, hoar, yellow	brown, darkish, green, pale, russet, verdant, yellow	embrowned, green, pale, russet, sable, verdant, yellow	black, brown, fiery brown, dark, dun, dusky, gilded, gray, green, dark green, deep green, wan green, hoary, iron, lurid, russet, sable, tawny, verdant, yellow
Terms for MOUNTAINS and HILLS				golden, green, hoary, gray	blue, gold	dusky, gray	bluish, hoary	blue, brown, dun, dusky, green, sable
Terms for DEEP WATERS				black, blue, green, wan	hoar, gray	green, yellow-gold	gray, green, hoar, pearl, silver	azure, black, blue, green, purple

COWPER	SCOTT	COLERIDGE	WORDSWORTH	BYRON	SHELLEY	KEATS
black	azure	amber	alabaster	azure	ashen	amethyst
blue	black	azure	azure	black	azure	azure
cerulean	blue	black	black	blue	black	black
gray	dark-blue	blue-black	blue	blush	blue	bloomèd
purple	blush	blue	black-blue	brazen	blush	blue
red	crimson	blush	dark-blue	crimson	cinereous	dark blue
rosy	dark	copper	sable-blue	dun	crimson	blush
	dusky	crimson	iron-brown	golden	dark	cerulean
	golden	ebon	cerulean	gray	ebon	crimson
	gray	golden	crimson	livid	emerald	dark
	pale	green	gilded	lurid	golden	dun
	pallid	yellow-green	golden	pale	green	ebon
	purple	gray	green	purple	sea-green	flushed
	red	lurid	gray	deep-purple	gray	golden
	blood-red	pale	lurid	red	iron	gray
	dark-red	pitchy	orange	dusky red	leaden	jet
	swarthy-red	purple	purple	rosy	livid	pale
	ruddy	red	purpureal	silver	orange	purple
	sable	dark-red	red	snowy	pale	rosy
	swarthy	rosy	rosy	white	pallid	roseate
	white	sapphire	roseate		pearl	sapphire
	yellow	wan	sapphire		purple	silver
		white	silver		dark purple	silver wan
			white		deepest "	white
			pearly white		red	
			yellow		blood-red	
					dark-red	
					rosy	
					roseate	
					ruddy	
					sanguine	
					sapphire	
					silver	
					snowy	
					vermilion	
					white	

COWPER	SCOTT	COLERIDGE	WORDSWORTH	BYRON	SHELLEY	KEATS
brown	black	black	black	brown	amber	amber
green	blue	brown	bronzed	black	azure	black
dark green	brown	dark	brown	dark	brown	blush
deep green	deeper brown	dusky	red-brown	emerald	chrysolite	brown
gilded green	dark	fiery	dark	gilded	crimson	dark
russet	dun	golden	darksome	golden	dark	dun
sable	emerald	green	dusky	green	dun	dusky
silver	gilded	dark green	emerald	dark green	dusky	emerald
tawny	gray	gray	fiery	dusky green	ebon	golden
verdant	green	pale	golden	hoar	emerald	green
wan	dark green	purpling	green	red	golden	sober gold
yellow	emerald-gr'n	red	gloomy "	scarlet	green	beechen-green
	light green	russet	grass "	verdant	dark green	dark green
	sepulchral "	silver	tawny "	yellow	sea-green	grass-green
	hoary	pinky-silver	gray		gray	light green
	pale	verdant	hoary		hoary	hazel
	purple	yellow	pale		livid	sable
	red		purple		pale	verdant
	dark red		purpureal		red	lily-white
	russet		red		verdant	yellow
	silver		russet		white	
	swarthy		sable		yellow	
	verdant		silver			
	yellow		verdant			
			white			

COWPER	SCOTT	COLERIDGE	WORDSWORTH	BYRON	SHELLEY	KEATS
azure	amethyst	green	azure	azure	black	black
green	blue	hoary	black	blue	blue	blue
	brown	rosy	blue	black	dark	light-blue
	crimson	verdant	brown	brown	green	green
	gray		dark	dark	gray	hoar
	hoary		dusky	dun	hoary	verdant
	purple		grain-	dusky	purple	
	sallow		green	gray	white	
	swarthy		hoary	green		
	white		purple	hoar		
			rosy-red	purple		
			rosy	verdant		
			verdant	white		
			white			
			yellow			

COWPER	SCOTT	COLERIDGE	WORDSWORTH	BYRON	SHELLEY	KEATS
green	azure	blue	azure	azure	amethystine	blue
white	black	cerulean	blue	black	azure	dark blue
	blue	dark	dark brown	blue	black	emerald
	dark blue	green	green	dark blue	blue	green
	livid blue	white	gray	deep blue	dark blue	blue-green
	dark		hoary	blushing	dark	gold-green
	dun		purpureal	dark	dusky	purple
	gold		silver	dun	emerald	
	green		white	dusky	glaucous	
	purple			golden	green	
	ruddy			gray	dark green	
	sable			green	gray	
	silver			deep green	hoary	
	snowy			hoar	pale	
	tawny			purple	purple	
	white			red	sapphire	
	silver-white			sapphire	silver	
				white	snowy	
					white	

www.ingramcontent.com/pod-product-compliance
Lightning Source LLC
Chambersburg PA
CBHW030610270326
41927CB00007B/1119